BLUE NOTE PREACHING
IN A POST-SOUL WORLD

BLUE NOTE PREACHING IN A POST-SOUL WORLD

Finding Hope in an Age of Despair

OTIS MOSS III

WESTMINSTER
JOHN KNOX PRESS
LOUISVILLE · KENTUCKY

© 2015 Otis Moss III

First edition
Published by Westminster John Knox Press
Louisville, Kentucky

15 16 17 18 19 20 21 22 23 24—10 9 8 7 6 5 4 3 2

Book design by Drew Stevens
Cover design by designpointinc.com
Cover photo by The All-Nite Images under the Creative Commons License

Library of Congress Cataloging-in-Publication Data

Moss, Otis.
  Blue note preaching in a post-soul world : finding hope in an age of despair / Otis Moss III. — First edition.
    pages cm
  ISBN 978-0-664-26160-3 (alk. paper)
  1. African American preaching. I. Title.
  BV4221.M67 2015
  251—dc23
                                                            2015031927

♾ The paper used in this publication meets the minimum requirements of the American National Standard for Information Sciences— Permanence of Paper for Printed Library Materials, ANSI Z39.48-1992.

*For Monica, who has been my muse
and the metronome of my heart.
You keep my heart beating to the rhythm of love.*

CONTENTS

Acknowledgments   ix
Introduction   xi

Chapter 1   THE BLUES MOAN AND THE
             GOSPEL SHOUT   1

Chapter 2   BLUES SENSIBILITY   22

Chapter 3   HIP-HOP ENGAGEMENT
             WITH A POSTMODERN WORLD   47

Sermon 1   LOVING YOU IS KILLING ME   66

Sermon 2   GAME OF THRONES   82

Sermon 3   MINISTRY AND OUR MANDATE   94

Sermon 4   HOW TO GET AWAY
             WITH MURDER   111

ACKNOWLEDGMENTS

There are several key people I must thank and give acknowledgment: Dean Gregory Sterling for the kind invitation to present the Lyman-Beecher lectures at Yale Divinity School. I cannot thank you enough for this grand and wonderful opportunity.

To my listening partner and spouse, Monica Moss. She read and listened to these lectures numerous times. She joked one day and said, "We gave the Beecher Lectures!" And it is true, *we* did! Thank you, Monica, for your hours of input, editorial suggestions, and love. None of this could have been possible without your support, your love, your kindness, and your humor.

I want to also thank my mother and father, Otis and Edwina Moss. My exposure to the voices of Gardner C. Taylor, Henry Emerson Fosdick, Howard Thurman, Sandy Ray, Samuel DeWitt Proctor, and many others came through their love of great preaching and, on road trips across the country, from hearing tapes of these marvelous ministers.

Thank you to my executive assistant, Melody Morgan, a woman who loves great writing. The conversations about Toni Morrison and Gloria Naylor were invaluable for this project. Not only the conversations, but your dedication to transcribe into a readable format my crazy notes and the pictures I created for this lecture.

I also want to thank two brilliant young preachers, the Rev. Neichelle Guidry-Jones and the Rev. Aaron McLeod. Rev. Neichelle offered phenomenal editorial work for the lecture, placing the lecture in Pages and Word with special notations for my review. Rev. McLeod, our director of Special Projects at Trinity United Church of Christ, made sure our Trinity community was "plugged in," praying and joining the pastor physically and virtually for these lectures.

Finally, I want to thank the people of Trinity United Church of Christ, a church with a long tradition of prophetic preaching solidified by my predecessor, the Rev. Dr. Jeremiah A. Wright, Jr. To the village of Trinity, I thank you for loving Monica, Elijah, Makayla, and myself and supporting us not only as we prepared for this event but also for the last seven years of ministry. You have taught me the power of grace, humor, and joy, and I thank you.

INTRODUCTION

The work and art of the preacher is a peculiar enterprise, often misunderstood and misinterpreted. The preaching art has been satirized in popular culture and shaded with demonic overtones by literary mavens who do not recognize the work of the preacher as a discipline and an art. Preaching has faced the judgment of academia and been marginalized by western culture, yet the word continues to go forth in various forms.

I grew up in a faith community where preaching and the preacher were respected as artists *and* academics, weaving together poetry and pragmatic wisdom for daily living. On Sunday mornings, I witnessed my father and pastor of the Olivet Institutional Baptist Church shape a new reality with metaphor, poetic rhythm, and intellectual engagement of philosophers. He stood week after week and dialogued with a text while he referenced Howard Thurman, Reinhold Niebuhr, Abraham Heschel, Fanny Lou Hamer, Khalil Gibran, Benjamin Elijah Mays, Constance Baker Motley, and Dorothy Day.

Each Sunday was a full meal of word, current affairs, Southern storytelling, and humor. Each week, my father created a message in which he struggled with great ideas and challenged us to question the world. He was raised in the segregated South, a pioneer in the Civil Rights Movement, organizer with the Atlanta Sit-In Movement, and a pastor. His theology and preaching introduced me to the importance of Blues and Jazz to the preaching project.

Black preaching, I believe, is more than preaching with a Black face; it is a unique cultural narrative and theological enterprise where African motifs meet diverse western influences of North America. A beautiful, bold, homiletical voice, poetry, prophetic witness, southern storytelling, lament, blues, and celebration are born out of this tradition.

Before his passing, I spent several consecutive summers with Dr. Fred Craddock, without a doubt, one of North America's homiletical luminaries. He served as Bible study teacher and theologian-in-residence for the Children's Defense Fund, Samuel DeWitt Proctor Conference of Child Advocacy at the Alex Haley Farm in Clinton, Tenn. A bunch of preachers, young and old, gathered around the lunch table daily to ask Dr. Craddock questions. He was gracious with his time and patient with us. I remember him remarking about the importance of Black preaching; "All preachers will do well to study the history, structure, and theology of the preached word that is birthed from the Black church." It was a quiet matter-of-fact comment coming from this intellectual giant, but it spoke to the yearning in my heart.

The preaching I heard as a boy and studied as an adult was not confirmed or ratified by seminaries or western gatekeepers. The preaching I witnessed danced with Lorraine Hansberry, did sets with John Coltrane, flowed with Maya Angelou, and was inspired by Langston Hughes. The preaching I heard seemed to know Amos personally, conversed with Isaiah weekly, and painted a picture of Jesus with such power that the aroma of wine at the wedding of Cana would saturate the air. The diversity of thought,

theology, and technique boggled my mind. Dr. Garner C.
Taylor, Dr. Martin Luther King Jr., Jarena Lee, Vernon
Johns, Ella Mitchell, Samuel DeWitt Proctor, Sandy Ray,
Lizzie Robinson, Esther Smith, William Seymour, William
Augustus Jones, C. L. Franklin, Miles Jones, Benjamin Eli-
jah Mays, and Prathia Hall. The list goes on, beyond the
time I have in this introduction.

During the Lyman-Beecher Lectures at Yale, I was
given the grand privilege to speak about not only preaching but also the magnificent and sometimes painful history
from whence Black, or "Blue Note," preaching is birthed.
The unique, brutal, yet sweet gift Black preaching gives to
the world is to allow the gospel to be viewed, once again,
from the eyes of those who sing Psalm 137:1-4 (NIV):

> By the rivers of Babylon we sat and wept
>   when we remembered Zion.
> There on the poplars
>   we hung our harps,
> for there our captors asked us for songs,
>   our tormentors demanded songs of joy;
>   they said, "Sing us one of the songs of Zion!"

> How can we sing the songs of the LORD
>   while in a foreign land?

A Blues aesthetic frees the preacher and preaching from
both personal-piety sermons and the ever-present prosper-
ity mode now popular on television. Blue Note preaching
seeks dialogue with Isaiah, Amos, Moses, the Woman at
the Well, a Gerasene demoniac and an imprisoned Paul.
Blue Note preaching dares to speak with love and creativity, "the world is not right, but God is still . . ."

This has and is a journey for me, and the work of these lectures has been a part of my life's working to bring the Blue Note back to the pulpit and reclaim the prophetic strand of a great tradition. I hope these lectures bless you. They were a joy to prepare and, I must say, I had a ball presenting them at Yale.

Asking you to imagine,
The Rev. Dr. Otis Moss III
May 2015

Chapter 1

THE BLUES MOAN
AND THE GOSPEL SHOUT

When the builders laid the foundation of the temple
of the LORD, the priests in their vestments were sta-
tioned to praise the LORD with trumpets, and the Levites, the sons of Asaph, with cymbals, according to
the directions of King David of Israel; ¹¹and they sang
responsively, praising and giving thanks to the LORD,
   "For he is good,
   for his steadfast love endures for ever toward
      Israel."
And all the people responded with a great shout
when they praised the LORD, because the foundation
of the house of the LORD was laid. ¹²But many of the
priests and Levites and heads of families, old people
who had seen the first house on its foundations, wept
with a loud voice when they saw this house, though
many shouted aloud for joy, ¹³so that the people
could not distinguish the sound of the joyful shout
from the sound of the people's weeping, for the people shouted so loudly that the sound was heard far
away. (Ezra 3:10–13)

I want to read this passage of scripture from a different version, the "OM3" version of Ezra—that's the Otis Moss III
version. Beginning with verses 11–12:

With praise and thanksgiving they sang to the Lord.
The Lord is good.
God's love toward Israel endures forever.
And all the people gave a great shout of praise to the
Lord, because the foundation of the house of the
Lord was laid. But many of the elders, the seasoned
saints, the older priests and Levites and family heads
who had seen the former Temple, wept aloud when
they saw the foundation of this Temple being laid.
While many others shouted for joy.

And here's the remix of verse 13:

No one could distinguish between the gospel shout
and the blues moan. No one could distinguish
between the gospel shout and the blues moan because
the people made so much noise. The sound could be
heard far away.

One generation shouting because they had not seen the
former. Another generation moaning because they remem-
bered what happened in the past. A generational paradox.
A challenge. One group trying to teach the blues. Another
group that was just ready to shout on Sunday. Here you
have this generational paradox wrapped up in this particular text. A blues moan and a gospel shout.

I contend that if we are to reclaim the best of the
preaching tradition then we must learn what I call the Blue
Note gospel. Before you get to your resurrection shout you
must pass by the challenge and pain called Calvary.

What is this thing called the *Blues*? It is the roux of
Black speech, the backbeat of American music, and the
foundation of Black preaching. Blues is the curve of the

Mississippi, the ghost of the South, the hypocrisy of the North. Blues is the beauty of Bebop, the soul of Gospel, and the pain of Hip-Hop.

Many academics have brilliantly placed Jazz in the conceptual motif of preaching. Both Eugene Lowery and Kirk Byron Jones brilliantly framed the importance of Jazz to the craft of preaching. Lowery's Beecher Lectures and book, *The Homiletical Beat,* take apart the elements of Jazz in relation to preaching. Jones gives a motif of engagement and pragmatic structure to preaching and preparing, with Jazz as the central idiom for homiletical development.

Frank A. Thomas, while not explicitly developing a homiletical theory of Jazz and preaching, implicitly pays homage to this enduring tradition through his classic book, *They Like to Never Quit Praisin' God: The Role of Celebration in Preaching.* Thomas masterfully connects celebration, theology, and the emotive process to African American culture and homiletical practice. Jazz is a backdrop to his work as he shares the power of reversals, sense appeal, and celebrative design.

All of these ideas are inherent in the construction of Jazz compositions. It is my task to give Blues her due and shed light on how she births a Jazz and Hip-Hop aesthetic of preaching.

Before we can speak of the Jazz mosaic or the Hip-Hop vibe for postmodern preaching, we must wrestle with the Blues. In his song "Call It Stormy Monday," T-Bone Walker laments how bad and sad each day of the week is, but "Sunday I go to church, then I kneel down and pray."

Walker's song unintentionally lifted up the challenge that the Blues placed before the church and that Black religiosity still seeks to solve. "Stormy Monday" forces the listener to reject traditional notions of sacred and secular.

The pain of the week is connected to the sacred service of Sunday. There is no strict line of demarcation between the existential weariness of a disenfranchised person of color and the sacred disciplines of prayer, worship, and service to humanity.

This Blue Note is a challenge to preaching and to the church. Can preaching recover a Blues sensibility and dare speak with authority in the midst of tragedy? America is living stormy Monday, but the pulpit is preaching happy Sunday. The world is experiencing the Blues, and pulpiteers are dispensing excessive doses of non-prescribed prosaic sermons with severe ecclesiastical and theological side effects.

The church is becoming a place where Christianity is nothing more than capitalism in drag. In his book, *Where Have All the Prophets Gone?*, Marvin McMickle, president of Colgate-Rochester Seminary, asks what happened to the prophetic wing of the church. Why have we emphasized a personal ethic congruent with current structures and not a public theology steeped in struggle and weeping informed by the Blues? McMickle's book is instructive for us; he demonstrates the focus on praise (or the neo-charismatic movements) coupled with false patriotism—enhanced by the reactionary development of the Tea Party, the election of President Barack Obama, and personal enrichment preaching (neo-religious capitalism informed by the market, masquerading as ministry).

The Blues has faded from the Afro-Christian tradition, and the tradition is now lost in the clamor of material blessings, success without work, prayer without public concern, and preaching without burdens. The Blues sensibility, not just in preaching, but inherent in American culture, must be recovered. We must regain the literary sensibility of Flannery O'Connor, Zora Neale Hurston, Ernest Hemingway, and James Baldwin; the prophetic speech of Martin Luther King Jr., William Sloane Coffin, and Ella Baker; along with the powerful cultural critique of Jarena Lee and Dorothee Solle.

The Blues, one of America's unique and enduring art forms, created by people kissed by nature's sun and rooted in the religious and cultural motifs of west Africa, must be recovered. The roots are African, but the compositions were forged in the humid Southern landscape of cypress and magnolia trees mingling with Spanish moss. It is more than music. The Blues is a cultural legacy that dares to see the American landscape from the viewpoint of the underside.

Ralph Ellison, the literary maven and cultural critic, states, "The blues is an impulse to keep the painful details and episodes of a brutal experience alive in one's aching consciousness. . . . As a form, the Blues is an autobiographical chronicle of personal catastrophe expressed lyrically" (Ralph Ellison and Robert G. O'Meally, *Living with Music: Ralph Ellison's Jazz Writings* [New York: Modern Library, 2001], 103).

My muse for understanding the Blues is rooted in two organic theologians and non-traditional homileticians, August Wilson and Zora Neale Hurston. This may sound strange. We are used to names rooted in the theological canon and given the stamp of approval by an elusive and sometimes mythical cabal of men whom we have never met, who give legitimacy to our thought. Both Wilson and Hurston capture the essence of Blues Speech and are chroniclers of Black religiosity and the healing power of God-talk, articulated by people who preach and sing in minor keys.

August Wilson, born Frederick August Kittel, Jr. in Pittsburg, Pennsylvania, is arguably America's most celebrated contemporary playwright, having created a cycle of ten plays for each decade of the twentieth century. Wilson's work is written with an overt Blues sensibility. He believed Blues Speech, carried by his characters and embodied by actors, has the power to save. For Wilson, speech wrapped up in the Blues is the antidote to the blues. The only way to get rid of your blues is to speak to your blues. It is his character, Ma Rainey, based on the real life Blues singer, Gertrude "Ma" Rainey, who speaks of the Blues' prophetic power to release the individual from spiritual isolation:

> The blues help you get out of bed in the morning. You get up knowing you ain't alone. There's something else in the world. Something's been added by that song. This be an empty world without the blues. I take that emptiness and try to fill it up with something. (August Wilson, *Ma Rainey's Black Bottom* [New York: New American Library, 1985], 83)

Ma Rainey becomes a prophetic preacher with a deep Blues sensibility. She is not seeking tragedy, but with a Womanist vibe and a Blues sensibility, she is stating, "I refuse to fall into despair."

Through Wilson, I learned, and the preacher learns, a new definition of preaching. Here it is: Blue Note preaching, or preaching with Blues sensibilities, is prophetic preaching—preaching about tragedy, but refusing to fall into despair. That is blues preaching. "And they could not distinguish between the gospel shout and the blues moan."

In his Beecher Lectures, Walter Brueggemann communicated that when we look at the Bible we must "Read, speak, and think as the poet." The academic or news reporter can neither understand the nuance nor conjure the power of prophetic Blues Speech.

Across the landscape of the cultural topography of America are reporters masquerading as prophets. You can hear them, can you not? They are announcing tragedy, sending notes of folly and foolishness, and crafting social-media posts of the decadence and demise of our culture. This is not prophetic Blues Speech; it is only shallow reporting and voyeurism, designed not to alter the world but to numb our spiritual senses. Over time we accept, when we hear this kind of speech, that the Real Housewives are actually real, even though everything they have is fake. That reality TV is authentic and anything shot on high definition video is a documentary. Blues Speech rescues us from acceptance and dares us to move from the couch of apathy to the position of work.

We view the world in multi-dimensional ways with Blues Speech and a Blues sensibility. We sing songs in major and minor keys and refuse to jettison lament from our vocabulary. The Blues dares us to celebrate all life and find the beauty in the midst of the magnificent mosaic of human contradiction. In Psalm 137, the psalmist speaks the Blues when the words go forth from the mouths of poets who speak with a Blues sensibility.

> By the rivers of Babylon, we sat down and wept
>   when we remembered Zion.
> There on the poplars
>   we hung up our harps,

for there our captors asked us for songs,
   our tormentors demanded songs of joy;
   they said," Sing us one of the songs of Zion!"

How can we sing the songs of the LORD
   while in a foreign land?

(vv. 1–4 NIV)

That is Blues Speech that gives reality to my reality, though I am not to speak about my reality. This is a
Blues song. This song of lament and celebration dares us
to speak of tragedy. August Wilson was informed by this
speech. His was biblical speech, translated through the lens
of Black culture. His work accurately portrays the power of
this type of communication. When we speak the Blues and
preach the Blues we connect with lost history and envision
a yet to be.

All of Wilson's plays create and envision a world that
royal speech, status quo speech, supremacist speech, cannot imagine. In this world, autonomous, artistic women
control their destinies, as in the person of Ma Rainey. In
this world, a mentally ill man, such as the character Gabriel
in Fences demonstrates that he may be the angelic messenger of God, disguised in mental illness. It is through August
Wilson that I am pulled into the world of the Blues, and
through Zora Neale Hurston that I find the power of prophetic conjuring.

Zora Neale Hurston, Harlem Renaissance writer,
folklorist, and novelist, spent her life recording the Blues
speech and patterns of displaced Africans. Her body of
work dares to claim that people of African descent do not
need external cultural validation; they have a rich culture,
whether or not it is acknowledged by Western scholars.

Hurston takes the speech of Southern storytellers, preachers, and singers, and peppers her fictional work with the wisdom gathered from these people, creating a rich tapestry of speech where Blues sensibilities and call-and-response moments are the norm. Hurston's famous novel, *Their Eyes Were Watching God,* gives a theological perspective informed by her Blues sensibility. The main character of the novel, Janie, who has taken hold of her destiny by marrying the much younger Teacake, seeks to find her place in the world. In one stunning section, Janie and Teacake take refuge from a hurricane and the Blues theology that Hurston has collected over the years emerges:

> "The wind came back with triple fury and put out the light for the last time. They sat in company with the others and other shanties, their eyes straining against crude walls and their souls asking if He meant to measure their puny might against His. They seemed to be staring at the dark, but their eyes were watching God." (Zora Neale Hurston, *Their Eyes Were Watching God* [Philadelphia: J. B. Lippincott Co., 1937], 191)

The preacher's call is to stand through storms after all the lights have gone out and the tourists have left the land. The call of the preacher is to stare in the darkness and speak the Blues with authority and witness the work of God in darkness and even in the abyss. Blues Speech and Blues theology change the gaze of the preacher. Flannery O'Connor calls this gaze the "grotesque in Southern fiction."

Christian writers, according to O'Connor, are burdened by the fact that they have knowledge of an alternative world because they have encountered a God of grace and love, but the world that they look at does not fit that which they have encountered. So there is a burden. This burden breaks forth from the fact that the writers know what the world should be, but they are burdened by the divine distance of humanity from divinity. Their gaze is cast upon what is called "the grotesque," those who are out of sync with God and characters that demonstrate the grace of God, though they have great distance from God. Through this tension, the writer is drawn to the grotesque of Blues and finds that God is loose in the world.

Isaiah, with poetic power and prophetic boldness, speaks with this same Blues sensibility. In Isaiah 10:1–2 (NIV), he says, "Woe to those who make unjust laws, / to those who issue oppressive decrees, / to deprive the poor of their rights / and withhold justice from the oppressed of my people, / making widows their prey / and robbing the fatherless." The prophet speaks with poetic language and lifts up the grotesque in the world of Israel. It is the prophet who points to the existential elements that lead to tragedy. In other words, he is speaking with a Blues sensibility of the policies of those in power, who create a lopsided, unjust world; the patriarchy of politicians who view women as objects for sport.

Isaiah, the poet and prophet, has the same eye and the same gaze and Blues sensibility of Billie Holiday singing "Strange Fruit":

> Southern trees bear strange fruit,
> blood on the leaves and blood at the root,
> black body swinging in the Southern breeze,
> strange fruit hanging from the poplar trees.
> (Lyrics from a poem titled "Strange Fruit"
> by Lewis Allan, 1937)

Billie Holiday is not singing to cause the audience to fall into despair but to empower all who hear. I will not allow you to cover your ears or your eyes. If we are to see a world that is different than the world that is now, I must speak the Blues. I must sing the Blues. Isaiah and Billie Holiday are doing the prophetic work of taking the covers off of oppression. When preachers refuse to preach, speak, and teach the Blues, they are knowingly tilling the ground for more strange fruit. The Blues is more than renaming of existential darkness; it is a way of seeing, a strategy of knowing, and a technique to empower.

Jesus is central to Blue Note preaching. It is Howard Thurman who speaks of how we must view Jesus as the liberator of the disinherited. In his classic text *Jesus and the Disinherited*, he speaks of Jesus as savior and liberator of those who have their backs against the wall. Scholar Obery Hendricks borrows from Thurman and expands our understanding of Jesus. In the powerful book *The Politics of Jesus*, Hendricks makes the compelling argument to view Jesus not solely as the sociological savior of oppressed people; but our normative view of Jesus must be of a person who lived life as a colonized individual. Jesus understands the pain of terrorism and is acquainted with the structures of disenfranchisement that rob people of their humanity.

In other words, Jesus knows all about our troubles.

The preached Word, when played, performed, and preached with the Blue Note sensibility, has the audacity to reclaim Jesus as Savior and liberator of marginalized people. The God of the Blue Note empowers men and women and refuses to be categorized by puny, inadequate definitions created by humans and concretized to and by the academy. It is the role of the prophet/preacher to harness a portion of this divine energy. The prophet seeks to paint a new world with the toolkit of oral performance, imagination, and keen intellectual investigation. In the process of painting this new world, the prophet is altered by the weight of the heavy elusive nature of the Word she or he carries. We cannot help but be bruised and blessed by the weight of the sacred task before us. The Word is so heavy that it leaves marks upon our shoulders, just as bruises were left upon the Israelites who carried the ark across the desert of Canaan. The Word cuts and leaves scars upon our body, fissures in our minds, as we seek to handle what cannot truly be handled.

Listen to the words of such a prophet, Maria Wright Stewart, schoolteacher, activist, and preacher. She was born into time in 1803 and born into glory in 1879. As a woman with a Blues sensibility, she was prescribed by society but redescribed by our God. Her oratory spoke unflinchingly of the horror of being a woman of African descent who was designed by God as a gift but mistaken by the world as a curse.

Hear the words of the prophet:

> The frowns of the world shall never discourage me nor its smiles flatter me; for, with the help of God, I am resolved to withstand the fiery darts of the devil, and the assaults of wicked men.
> (*Meditations from the Pen of Mrs. Maria W. Stewart* [Washington, DC: W. Lloyd Garrison & Knapp, 1879], 60)

Blue Note preaching is a way of knowing. We refuse to turn away from the beauty in the ashes; neither shall we turn from the ashes that were once a bouquet of beauty: *I am African, I am black, I am woman, I am displaced; yet I pull from my sacred toolkit a palette of colors capable of beautifying the decaying walls of my prison.* In the process of preaching, we unlock the gates of the prison with a word the world cannot comprehend.

As a child, I loved a particular cartoon that appeared on the Captain Kangaroo show. The cartoon was entitled "Simon," and to this day I still am able to recite a portion of the theme song: "I know my name is Simon . . . for the things I draw come true."

Simon was a simple stick-figure cartoon character living in a colorless, drab world. I watched Simon pull out his piece of chalk and begin to draw a new world on the backdrop of his desolate life. Streets were formed, doors were created, and ships were produced, taking him off to new countries and worlds untouched by any being. Simon's imagination was the doorway out of his drab existence. When he harnessed the power of what was placed in him by his creator/illustrator, he was able to create a new world.

James Weldon Johnson's classic *God's Trombones* is rooted in this simple task of the preacher's role to create a new world with words, tones, dynamics, and a Blues sensibility. The artistic construction inherit in the sermon and the collective consciousness of the people create a healing moment to reconnect the fractured personality of a community traumatized by the institution of human trafficking known as slavery.

The preacher who is armed with the Word and shaped by the Blues is able to create a new world in the face of an old world that denies the humanity of people of color. Listen to James Weldon Johnston:

> And God stepped out on space,
> and he looked around and said:
> I'm lonely—
> I'll make me a world.
>
> ("The Creation," *God's*
> *Trombones* [New York:
> Viking Press, 1927], 17)

Johnson viewed the preacher as an artist and healer with the power to create through an imagination touched by the divine.

The preacher functions like the cartoon character Simon, Weldon's poetry, and the prophet Isaiah: they draw with the paintbrush of the Word, strokes of tone, colors of oratory, auditory dynamics on a drab canvas of a broken world. Christ brings colors, tone, dynamics, chords, and a new time signature to the world.

You can hear, can you not, the sounds of women and men who had the smell of mud, manure, and magnolia on their feet. They stand with dignity as cool red clay presses between their toes and the unforgiving southern sun beats them with a continual whip of heat and humidity. Can you not see upon these unknown black bodies, tendons stretched beyond capacity and muscles bulging under the weight of rice, cotton, and tobacco? Somewhere between insanity and despair a new music is born: spirituals, ring shouts, and work songs, coupled with an oratorical dexterity the world had never seen!

Can I get a witness!

An entire orchestra was birthed "down by the riverside" as mothers sang "roll, Jordan, roll." A new speech, with conjuring power infused with an anointing that the West claimed did not exist, had stepped into the light. The

Blue Note and Blues sensibility was born in this place of death that became the place of life. Just as Jesus hung up on the cross and transformed an execution into a celebration, the Blue Note sensibility conjured life from death's domain. The Blue Note is the Africanization of a faith that forgot its roots. The Blue note turns the gospel back to Jesus, the church back to Christ, and the preacher back to the prophets. Christianity was a prisoner of markets, manifest destiny, and men, until the Blues set it free to see Christ, Calvary, and the cross once again.

The Blues, or Blue Note preaching, performed by the artist of African descent, brings a new vitality to the act of the performed word and structure of homiletics. Preachers of African descent were born outside of the American project, forced to gaze through the window of democracy. They yearned and wept for strange gifts that were on display on the other side of the windowpane, gifts with strange names, such as "freedom," "democracy," "free agency," "autonomy," and "humanity," and the list goes on. This distance and yearning gave the preacher of African descent a "second sight."

The preacher entered the pulpit and stepped up to the lectern with an eye upon the existential tragedy manufactured by a false anthropology and demented theology. The preacher witnessed a country claiming equality yet birthed in the blood of a holocaust of red and black bodies. The preacher—nursed upon the breast of inhumanity, yet raised on the promise of Christ's eternity—is given a second sight, born with a veil or "caul" upon her or his spirit.

Southern tradition claims that children born with a veil were "called," or given a second sight; a glimpse into the unseen world of ancestors, haunts, ghosts, prophecy, and God talk. Blue Note preaching has, for lack of a better phrase, a "Duboisian" nature that allows it to penetrate the stronghold of American myth and embody the scripture with a renewed vitality rarely witnessed on these shores. Blue Note preaching does not appropriate biblical stories but embodies the Word.

The text lives and inhabits the breath and body of the preacher and people. For example, Moses is not appropriated as a liberator or a stand-in for people of color. Moses is African sociologically. Moses is African theologically. Moses is African metaphorically; and yes, Moses is African literally (the brother was straight out of Egypt). He ceases to be the Charleston Heston or Christian Bale myth and inhabits the bodies of Harriet Tubman, Martin Luther King Jr., and Vernon Johns. The spirit of Moses transcends gender reassignment in the Blue Note tradition. Heston played Moses on film. Tubman conjured Moses in the flesh. This embodied action, born in the crucible of American cruelty, produced an ability to see beyond the mythos of the empire and to breathe life into the text.

There was nothing like witnessing, not just the preacher becoming possessed by the Word, but the entire congregation reshaping the message as they affirm, push, doubt, and support the preacher, with words such as, "Take your time," and "That's Right!" and with the assent of the preacher. Every stroke of the call and response etches a new message in the lived experience of the congregation. Whatever was written on paper is reshaped and reformed in the moment it is performed and presented before the people.

This second sight gives Blue Note preaching a unique perspective. Blue Note preaching is not completely African, yet it is rooted in West African motifs. It is not European, yet much of what it is has elements of Europe. It is American, a

Creole style and aesthetic that has the power to unhinge the American empire. Blue Note preaching has shaken foundations and toppled governments across the ages.

It is Martin Luther King Jr. and his very words—whether on the Mall in DC in 1963, or at Riverside Church when he broke the silence and came out against the war in Vietnam—that not only caused the Senate, Congress, and White House to take notice, but also caused the FBI to work overtime to destroy and disrupt the nonviolent Civil Rights Movement. Is it not strange and a peculiar irony that America places a monument in Washington, DC, to a small Southern preacher who pastored a church in Montgomery, Alabama, that could not seat more than 250 people? A stone was etched to create the figure of Martin Luther King Jr., and it now stands watch over Thomas Jefferson, George Washington, and Abraham Lincoln to ensure that the "yet to be United States of America" shall live up to its creed. This is the power of Blue Note preaching.

When we look at Blue Note elements biblically, we see that Moses found his power in this second sight. He possessed an intimate knowledge of Egyptian culture, from having been a student of Amen-Ra. He knew the Ivy League culture of the Egyptian mystery system. Yet he was still a child of Abraham. Moses had second sight, a veil giving his soul the power to see the true nature of the empire. Moses was what people in New Orleans call a "creole child." He can recite the story of Abraham and sing the songs of Osiris. This section of his resume causes the heavens to take notice. He knows the pain of oppression and the comfort of the empire. It is Vernon Johns who stated, and I paraphrase, "When Moses hit the Egyptian upside the head with that brickbat, all of the heavens took note and God pointed and said, "Get me that young man. He knows about the pain of oppression and he knows about the comfort of the empire. He shall lead my movement."

Moses was Ivy League and urban league, Mozart and Mos Def, Handel and WC Handy, Rachmaninoff and Ma Rainey. His ability to understand the empire and still be faithful to his God was the root of his revolutionary power. "To be from but not of" is a unique burden and blessing. I recall Maya Angelou referring to it as sweet brutality; to love the sweetness but yet know that you cannot be released from the brutality.

W. E. B. Dubois puts it this way,

> "The Negro is sort of a seventh son, born with a veil, and gifted with-second sight in this American world,—a world which yields him no true self-consciousness, but only lets him see himself through the revelation of the other world. It is a peculiar sensation, this double-consciousness, this sense of always looking at one's self through the eyes of others, of measuring one's soul by the tape of a world that looks on in amused contempt and pity. (*The Souls of Black Folk* [Chicago: A. C. McClurg & Co., 1903], 3)

This is the tragic roux that is stirred at the bottom of the pot of Blue Note preaching.

I see two worlds. I witness the schizophrenic nature of American pathology, and I know a remedy for the spiritual bifurcation in my soul, and that remedy is Jesus. Jesus is so central to Blue Note preaching that it is accused of being Christocentric. Jesus ceases to be a past historical figure, a mere theological idea or textural object for examination. Quite the contrary—Jesus is real.

Jesus knows all about my troubles.
Jesus walks and talks with me.
Jesus picks me up and turns me around and plants my feet
    on solid ground!
Jesus is a mind regulator,
    a heart fixer,
    a friend at midnight,
    balm in Gilead,
    trouble over deep water,
    and bread in a starving land.
Jesus understands my predicament.

Why does he understand my predicament?

Jesus lived a life as a colonized person and as a minority in
    a community that was under siege by an occupying army.
Jesus understands poverty created by an empire,
Jesus knows about racial profiling,
Jesus understands mass incarceration,
Jesus is frustrated with the traditional church,
Jesus experiences state sponsored torture,
    knows what it's like to have a public defender who lacks
        competency,
    was executed for a crime he did not commit
    and understands character assassination in the media
        before and after one's death.
Jesus even knows what it is like to be stopped and frisked.
Jesus is acquainted with patriarchy,
    since not a single brother would listen to any of the
        sisters when they announced,
"Guess what y'all, the tomb is empty!"
Jesus knows all about our troubles . . .
Jesus wrestles with tragedy but does not fall into despair.

Jesus is on the cross at that Blue Note moment but does not fall into despair. He forces us to face the tragedy. Then, as the old preachers would say, a few days later, "Early on Sunday morning, Jesus got up with all power in his hands . . ."

But here is the thing, the one who taught me most about Blue Note preaching was a little girl about six years of age, my daughter, Makayla.

Trinity Church went through a very painful and challenging moment as my predecessor was unfairly lifted up and attacked in the media because there was a person who had been kissed by nature's sun who was running for the presidency. As a result, we had media outside every day. There were death threats, at least a hundred every week: "We are going to kill you. We are going to bomb your church."

You want to keep that sort of thing away from your family, but the stress was so painful, it made it very difficult to sleep at night. I remember one night I was half asleep and heard some noise in the house. My wife, Monica, punched me and said, "*You* go check that out" [Oh yes, it's okay to laugh]. So I did. Just like a good preacher, I grabbed my rod and staff to comfort me. I went walking through the house with my rod and staff that was made in Louisville with the name "Slugger" on it.

I looked downstairs, and then I heard the noise again, and I made my way back upstairs and peeked in my daughter's room. There was a six-year-old girl dancing in the darkness . . . just spinning around, saying, "Look at me, Daddy."

I said, "Makayla, you need to go to bed. It is 3:00 a.m. You need to go to bed."

But she said, "No, look at me, Daddy. Look at me."

And she was spinning; barrettes going back and forth, pigtails going back and forth.

I was getting huffy and puffy wanting her to go to bed, but then God spoke to me at that moment and said, "Look at your daughter! She's dancing in the dark. The darkness is around her but not in her. But she's dancing in the dark."

If you dance long enough, weeping may endure for a night, but joy will come in the morning. It is the job of every preacher to teach the congregation to dance in the dark. Do not let the darkness find its way in you, but dance in the dark.

May God bless you. May God keep you. But dance. Dance! Dance!

Click here for the original lecture video.

Chapter 2

BLUES SENSIBILITY

In chapter 1, we examined the Blues and discussed what Blue Note preaching is. It is preaching about tragedy but not falling into despair. We focused on that text in Ezra where there was a Gospel shout and there was a Blues moan. A Blue Note sensibility is the merging of this shout and moan. I believe that we are called to regain this sensibility in this postmodern and post-Soul age if we are to preach prophetically. This chapter looks at the idea of Blues, beginning from a different vantage point.

There is a story passed from mouth to ear by Southern graves from the palmetto trails of South Carolina—the Lowcountry, as it is called—somewhere on the island of St. John. A mythic tale of truth was born, bound by the nostalgic hyperbole that is rooted and fertilized by the soul of displaced, transatlantic Africans. No one knows the exact origin of this tale. The details seem to differ with the writer or teller. But the meaning always remains the same. This tale was forged somewhere between the wisdom of West Africa and the tragedy of American slavery. It is the story of a people who could fly.

The tale begins on the island of St. John, as displaced Africans who had been mislabeled as slaves toiled in the hot sun under the devious watchful eye of a nameless slave driver. Among this group of coffee black, mocha brown, and caramel colored people was a woman tending her child and picking cotton. She had such dexterity that she could pick cotton with her right hand and caress the forehead of her child with her left. She was picking cotton, exhausted from the pressure of working in the humid conditions, when her body gave out under the stress and weight. When W. E. B. Dubois told the story, he described her fall by saying that she collapsed from the weight of being a problem and property all at the same time. Her strong yet frail body simply collapsed under the weight of waking up every day to face the tragedy and the absurdity of a people who claimed to be Christian but always lived in contradiction. This woman, this nameless woman, fell to the ground and her boy, who could have been no more than six or seven, attempted to wake his mother from this disoriented state, knowing that if the slave masters were to witness this sudden stop in work, punishment would be swift and hard.

The slave drivers noticed that the woman had fallen under their gaze in the shadow of the cotton, and they climbed their beasts of burden to ride to the place where she had disappeared. They moved across the field, but before the drivers could reach her, an old man came over to the woman who had fallen. The people called him "Preacher" or Prophet" but the slave master called him "Old Devil." The little boy looked into the kind face of this old man and simply asked, "Is it time?" The old man just smiled and nodded and uttered one word in the woman's ear and the same word into the boy's ear, "*Kulibah!*" The woman miraculously gained strength when the word entered her ear and landed on her spirit. As a matter of fact, the other Africans stopped working to witness the birth of a queen, for at that moment she rose from the ground. She looked toward the slave drivers who were riding on their beasts of burden toward her, and she looked at her son. She grasped his hand; they both looked up toward Heaven and began to fly. The slave drivers lost their composure, unable to process this idea of human flight.

During their brief moment of disbelief, Preacher ran to the other slaves and told them, "It's time!" He began to utter, "Kulibah, kulibah, kulibah!" The Africans rose from the fields, and their flight to freedom began. Can you imagine this sight; the dehumanized flying, three fifths of a person flying, the disenfranchised flying, the dishonored flying, the disempowered flying, the discouraged flying, the dismissed flying, the dismembered flying, the disadvantaged flying, the diseased flying, the disinherited flying, the dislocated flying? All taking flight with such grace and beauty to a world no one had yet seen.

The slave drivers grabbed the old man and beat him to within an inch of his life. They interrogated him, but the more they beat him the more he smiled, with blood flowing from his brow. The slave masters demanded that he bring back the slaves. The old man just looked at them, smiled, and simply said, "I can't. Once the word is in them, it will never leave them."

The old man was given an ancient word. He was a steward of the mysteries. The word *Kulibah* originated on the shores of West Africa and literally means "God is in you." He did not create it, he just spoke it. The prophet did not keep the word, he did not create it. He just passed on to someone else the word that was given to him. He did not hoard the word. He passed on the word so that someone else could be freed by this word. He did not own it, no.

There is something about the old man, this preacher, that reminds every woman and man who is called by God of what we must do. We are not called to make people shout. We are not called to make people dance. We are not called to make people feel good. We are not called to preach what people want to hear. We are called to give a *Kulibah* word, a word that will move in one's spirit so that people will take flight, fly from their breakdowns to a breakthrough. In the words of my father, they will move from disgrace and move to dignity. They will fly from being broken to recognizing that they are a blessing from God.

We are called to place a word in people. We do not own it. We did not create it. We are called to be a conduit for a *Kulibah* word that transforms people to a new level. This is the power of Blue Note preaching. It is a *Kulibah* word that, in the words of my father again, moves people "from disgrace to dignity." And the *Grio*, the Preacher, who has been charged to tell the story, uses her dynamic imagination and interpretive lens to create an alternative world in the collective mind of the village. The Grio, through the story, is saying, "tragedy will not have the last word. Despair will not engulf my soul." The Grio carries a healing medicine formed from the silence of resonance of breath and vibration. *Kulibah*, the word has power. Just as the Word becomes flesh, the Word has power, and if we want this generation to take flight, if we desire for preaching to continue to empower people to fly, we must move back with a *Sankofa* spirit, that is fetch what is at risk of being left behind and reclaim the Blue Note power of preaching.

The task of the preacher is to wrestle with the Blue Note of life and find the assurance of grace in the gospel. Blue Note preaching requires a different hermeneutic. The preacher is required to do the academic work, the exegetical digging. All of these are tools, but the preacher is required to submit to the Spirit and be possessed by Divine imagination.

The Blue Note preacher views the preaching task as art. Words are the preacher's craft, like the paintbrush of the painter and the instrument of the composer. This is art, not technical precision: art, deeply expressed through the personality of the preacher. Thomas Merton gives a definition of art that is applicable to preaching: "Art enables us to find ourselves and lose ourselves at the same time" (Thomas Merton, *No Man Is an Island* [New York: Harcourt, Brace and Co., 1955], 35).

Blue Note preaching is the creation of an alternative world and an alternative consciousness. As the story of "The People Who Could Fly" illustrates, the preacher breathes a Word into the people and they are found. They are given life, and they rise above the degradation of the plantation. The story is also a story of being consumed by power beyond oneself. The people fly and disappear, never to be heard of again. The Word gives them agency, but they are also carried away to a land conceived of only in their imaginations.

The imagination of the story gives eschatological hope while staring at existential darkness: *"I'm on the plantation, but I'm not of the plantation. When the Word is in me I'm ready to return home."*

The task of the preacher who seeks to recover a Blues sensibility must be to create a hermeneutic that views the text with an artistic eye and a Blues lens. This is not a new idea; it is one that has been lifted and learned down through the ages. The poet, the artist, the dancer, the writer, and the Hebraic prophet understand the need for metaphor, symbol, double entendre, image, and sound. We cannot encounter the Holy with easy definitions; nor can we engage people with words and images with a singular meaning. We need a *Kulibah* word, a word with multiple definitions, which, when it is spoken, births new meaning. The Blues lens for hermeneutical interpretation offers a wider pallet of colors to the preacher who is attempting to paint in a postmodern world that is addicted to ease, empire, and markets.

Jerome Clayton Ross, assistant professor of Old Testament at the Samuel Dewitt Proctor School of Theology at Virginia Union University, shares a powerful view of the implications of this type of hermeneutic for preaching. "Except for the reign of David through Solomon, the Yahwists were dominated by super power nations during the biblical period . . . these nations superimposed their cultures upon the nations or peoples whom they ruled, thereby establishing the standards of living for them" (Samuel K. Roberts, *Born to Preach: Essays in Honor of the Ministry of Henry and Ella Mitchell* [Valley Forge, PA: Judson Press, 2000]). Ross goes on to share the six kingdoms that imposed a form of colonialism upon the Hebrew people: Egypt, Assyria, Babylon, Persia, Greece, and Rome. This has profound implications for preaching. If we are to recover a Blues sensibility, we must have the audacity to read the Bible with a Blue Note lens, understand the Blues inherent in the Bible, and preach what we read.

The hermeneutic for the Blue Note homiletic seeks contextualization and artistic imagination, drawn from engagement with scripture and deep, abiding spirituality. The preacher uses all the tools at her disposal, working to understand context in light of the limited freedom and agency of an ancient people and communicating grand theological ideas of the gospel. Through the merging of artistic imagination we are given a broader understanding, of not only the text but also the activity of God.

Artistic imagination, in the words of Eugene Lowry, is "dancing the edge of mystery"(*The Sermon: Dancing the Edge of Mystery* [Nashville: Abingdon Press, 1997]). Artistic imagination, in the words of Dr. Lenora Tubbs-Tisdale of Yale Divinity School, is "rekindling the fire within" (*Prophetic Preaching* [Louisville, KY: Westminster John Knox Press, 2010], 21) as defines this act. Father Mapple, Herman Melville's character from *Moby Dick*, tells us, "Woe to him whom this world charms from Gospel duty!" ([New American Library, 1892], 50). The artistic imagination gives over to the world a Blues sensibility to create a new world for the preacher.

I want to give you some of this idea of artistic imagination. As I dipped my pen into ink in my own sanctified imagination, I was able to write a Blues song. In dealing with David, the preacher's/priest's role is to play the Blues in public space. The people join in the song and acknowledge the story, and they even place embers upon the fire of atonement. The story of David and Bathsheba is a story I like to call, simply, "The Rooftop Blues." It speaks to the eternal tragedy of human folly, nurtured by our gluttonous egos. While on the rooftop, David gazes upon the body of a woman who ceases, in his eyes, to have agency:

David's gaze is cast against the stone skyline of the kingdom. He breathes a deep breath and exhales, and wonders how his men are faring in their campaign. Triumph has become an expectation for him. The late-night pacing has been replaced by elusive moments of anxiety, which are quickly dispelled by the history of triumph, and the otherworldly promise of his God.

He is king, raised from the barrio of Bethlehem, dismissed by all, including his own father, who didn't think he could become a king. The thought that he could be wanted and valued by God as a leader was absurd to his father. The thought brings an ironic smile to David's face, not of joy, but of sadness. His father never believed he had the ability to lead. In his parental consciousness, David would forever chase the smell of wool and manure in the fields and Bethlehem.

Until the day the prophet showed up and a wide vision was cast through the narrow window of Bethlehem.

David always had more heart than strength and was willing to face any bully on the playground or the battlefield, as was the case with Goliath. He is king now, but he cannot erase the light ache in his heart. He will always be the boy from Bethlehem, the little barrio shepherd with country ways, who could not erase the stench of wool and manure from his skin.

As he continues to look across the horizon of his city, his eyes rest upon a rooftop. The sun dances across the black skin of a woman bathing in a tiny tub. Not realizing his mouth was slightly opened, he imagines his next campaign as he stares.

The preacher, when staring into the story of David, must refuse to be sentimental. The Blue Note of interpretation pushes aside a Sunday-school faith and calls the preacher/prophet to dance to the rhythm of the Blues. We recognize our humanity and contradiction in David. We witness our folly and see God lurking in the corners as a metaphysical narrator. The preacher must resist the call to edit for acceptability and dare to speak tragedy before the people who want to forget, but they must remember in order to be healed.

When the prophet dares to expose to the light the congregation who is living in darkness, the initial reaction is to wince in pain. Our eyes have adjusted to the dark. Our world has been designed by shadows, not truth. The preacher causes pain, but slowly, very slowly, we adjust to the light, and in our adjustment, we see David, Tamar, Absalom, and Amnon. We see fathers, sisters, brothers, aunts, and cousins. If the gaze is cast long enough, we witness structures, ideological myths, and duets with demons, with whom we cowrote songs that are on heavy rotation in our consciousness with people who seek to destroy who we are.

Almost every year at Trinity, I deal with a text of terror. One particular text of terror that I always have to deal with—because she sat down next to me one time in my imagination—is a sister by the name of Tamar. Normally, especially within our tradition, you've got to have some good news when you preach. When you're talking about Tamar, though, there ain't no good news up in that one. But as I had a conversation with Tamar, she simply asked me, "Just do this, Otis, just tell my story to the church."

It is very important that a man say the story because it was the pulpit and patriarchy that crushed so many sisters. To have the opportunity to share her story as I stood before the congregation, I said to Tamar—every Tamar—we are sorry we did not speak up for you. We did not call your name. We allowed patriarchy, peculiar ideas for next level blessings, to overtake our theology. We are sorry for not telling your story.

As I stood before the people and Tamar whispered in my ear, I told the story, Tamar's story. I said, it was not your fault. I let them know there was collusion between a cousin and a brother who violated you. But the real violation was not just what happened with Amnon and Jonadab, the cousin of Amnon; the real violation was that your daddy didn't say anything. How do you recover from the fact that your father is silent, but your father knew?

The question was, where is this good news? Tamar did something with a womanist ethic, with a liberation perspective. She said, "David, since you won't speak for me, I'm going to go ahead and speak for myself. I will not use words. I'm just going to change my clothes. I'm going to put on sackcloth and ashes. I know that you are a political fellow, and you want everyone to think everything is all right in the palace. They will see me walking with my sackcloth and ashes, and there will be whispers in Israel, "All is right in the kingdom."

As we communicated, and as Tamar talked in my ear, there was a particular imaginative revelation that happened at that moment that said, yes, you must put on sackcloth and ashes; but Tamar whispered and said, "I wore them for a good portion of my life. Tell everyone in the church, make sure they have a change of clothes. Wear your sackcloth. Know that there was pain and violation, but do not let that define who you are. At some point you must change your clothes."

As I shared the story of Tamar, I also opened my heart to the congregation and shared the story of my sister Daphne. My sister struggled for years with mental illness. Unfortunately, she now watches over me from the battlements of Heaven. Her struggle with schizophrenia, voices, and paranoia became too much for her, and she eventually took her own life four days before my wedding. This tragic episode demanded I either succumb to the Blues or learn to sing the Blues. The reason that I am able to stand here before you and talk about Zora Neale Hurston and James Baldwin and Langston Hughes and all of those with a Blues sensibility is because at the age of four, five, six, and seven, instead of reading me Dr. Seuss, my sister read Zora Neale Hurston to me. And so it was always in my spirit. By the time I got to college, I already had Zora imprinted on my soul, but I didn't even know it until the teacher started talking. I said, I know who she is, because that was my bedtime story as a child.

I remember when my sister came home from Spelman one summer, and she was feeling sad. My room was next to hers, and she was crying. She was crying because someone had treated her bad. I was nine years old, and I said, "Tell me where the brother is, I'll take care of him. I'm your little brother, that's what brothers do. We take care of things."

She said, "No, that's alright, there's nothing you can do."

I said, "Well you just let me know. I will roll! I will get on my bike, and I will roll! Whatever I gotta do, I will do it!"

She said, "No, don't worry about it, everything is okay."

So she was depressed for a good portion of the summer. I would hear her crying at night. Then one night I heard her snapping her fingers. She was shouting and having a good time. I said, "Daphne, what's going on? You've been crying all summer."

She said, "Well, the Lord removed the Blues from me, took away the pain."

I asked, "How did that happen?"
She said, "I was listening to the radio."
I said, "What happened?"

She said, "I heard a song."

I asked, "Did some Gospel song come on?"

She said, "No, no. I was listening to some 'old school' songs, and a disco song came on."

I said, "The Lord does not speak through disco!"

She said, "No, no, no; I'm telling you a disco song changed my life."

I said, "What happened?"

She said, "Sometimes God will send prophets in other kind of ways, and I was listening to these old school songs when a sister by the name of Gloria Gaynor came on—a song called "I Will Survive."

And my sister proceeded to sing the words to "I Will Survive," that she had been afraid, petrified, after she'd been done wrong, wondering how she could get along. But then she got strong and realized she could survive. As long as she knows how to love, she's got all her love to give. She would survive!

As I presented that story on a particular Sunday, the congregation began to sing the song. The musicians joined in. All of a sudden we were singing "I Will Survive," and it became an invitation to the altar. The women who had been violated but were now victors came to the altar, but not facing the altar, facing the congregation, and they said, "I will pray with you." And they prayed together, and they began to build prayer partnerships to let us know, "I've been where you are, and I am here to walk with you to set you free."

When the preacher refuses to edit for accessibility, God can speak in a way that God does not speak when you have the abridged version of the gospel.

The prophetic gaze is a Blue Note gaze that dares to shatter and reshape the world. The preacher must approach the text, not with forensic distance, but with artistic passion. The lives of the people, the world of the story, and the pain of the characters must encroach on the consciousness of the preacher and the people. The artistic approach looks at the Bible as a living Word, not a dead scroll. Our lives are swirling between the lines, from and on the lips of the men and women of the text. A mirror is pushed to the surface from beneath the dust, dirt, and sand, covering from time period to time period.

We are reunited with ourselves. We become like Dorian Gray inspecting his own portrait, painted by Basil Hallward (see Oscar Wilde, *The Picture of Dorian Gray*, 1890). Dorian Gray noticed that his portrait carried every sin, crime, and violation he had perpetrated. In our portraits, we notice that sin, sanctimonious self-righteousness, and arrogance have corrupted a beautiful, divinely drawn picture of humanity. The person we think we are is not congruent with the figure in the painting. Every cruelty, rebellion, unethical act, and amoral position is recorded on our canvases.

The preacher paints with a homiletical brush upon a spiritual canvas. The courage of the preacher rests in this artistic danger. The artist/preacher is always at risk of rejection by a people who wrongfully believe that they have called and commissioned the preacher to paint a flattering family portrait to be hung in the northwest corridor of their hearts. What a danger to preach; for preaching brings the purveyor into contact with a world of conflict and contradiction.

Those who see themselves as patrons, and not parishioners, will seek to destroy and discredit the artist, the preacher, the prophet for painting a portrait that dares show the ugly tragedy that is held in the lives of ordinary women and men.

Many who hear and read the Blues misinterpret the songs as sorrow meditations, music designed to focus on suffering and boxed in by narrow anthropology. I say no. Blues is a celebration. After one has found a new Blue Note hermeneutic and dares to reach into the imagination with an artistic lens, something happens. What from the outside looks like sorrow is turned into unspeakable joy. This seems like an impossibility, but joy comes from the Blues. There is no shouting like the shouting in a Black church about the resurrection of Jesus Christ. As a matter of fact, you can say the same thing every week. "They hung Him high. They stretched Him wide, and then He died. But early on Sunday morning, before the rooster started to crow . . ." (adapted from David Allen, "No Greater Love"). Every week you can say the same thing, because it is the retelling of a story, a narrative. But the joy and the shouts heard on Sunday morning are deeply tied to the Blues of Good Friday. Sunday morning is impossible to conceive without the Blues of Calvary. You cannot get to that moment of a shout without dealing with the pain of Friday.

Scholar and iconic activist Angela Davis brilliantly defines the power of speaking and singing the Blues. Blues singers, especially women, use the Blues to reorient the psyche after the disorientation of patriarchy and racialized oppression. Ma Rainey, Bessie Smith, and Billie Holiday preached through song. Their words created a world where women were empowered. All three used voice, sound, song, and speech to connect to a spirituality informed by Africa and shaped by America. I like how Bessie Smith says it:

It may be a week,
it may be a month or two
but the day you quit me honey,
it's coming home to you.

                    Alberta Hunter,
              "Down Hearted Blues"

The Blues became an empowering mechanism for Bessie Smith, Ma Rainey, and Billie Holiday. The power of Blues or Blue Note sensibility cannot be completely written down. Stephen H. Webb calls this "a theology of sound, or theo-acoustic engagement" (*The Divine Voice: Christian Proclamation and the Theology of Sound* [Eugene, OR: Wipf & Stock, 2012]). Preaching is an oral art, not a written form. We're not reading essays from the pulpit, y'all. It is rooted in sound; the dynamics of the voice. That is your paintbrush. That is your tool that you use. Whatever that sound may be, whether it is a dynamic, high, loud, booming voice, whatever, use what God gave you. It is rooted in sound.

Preaching is not words on paper. It is performed; but when I say *performance*, I do not speak of entertainment. Performance is an act of preaching, not entertainment. It is the act of the experiential embodiment of an idea, using all sensory resources to communicate to another person. It is fascinating, especially in certain traditions; people will raise the question, even have raised it with me: "Why do you communicate that way? You seem so excited when you communicate." Yes, I am, I'm talking about Jesus! Jesus is worth being excited about! So it makes complete sense to be excited. But there is an embodiment that happens when something is deeply resonating in your spirit and in your soul. Musicians do it all the time. If you watch Miles

Davis, he expresses his music through physicality and musicality. If you look at Thelonious Monk, sometimes he has to spin around. Every preacher has that particular embodiment. When I watch my father when he preaches, he will grab his lapels. When I see Freddie Haynes preach, he will spread his arms wide. When I see Michael Dyson preach, he'll start moving his hands. When I see Johnny Ray Youngblood preach, he will throw his hands . When Dr. Cynthia Hale preaches, she'll put that hand on her hip and just start going! There is embodiment to preaching and something happens. It is not just your voice. It's your entire being. Everything should be used when you are presenting that which is holy, that which is elusive. You must use your voice and use your mind, use your heart, use your spirit, use your body, because it is an artistic dance happening before the people.

Preaching is an act of performance. Preaching uses all of the dynamics of communications, and Blue Note preaching especially takes culture into consideration to communicate.

Dr. Teresa Fry-Brown of Emory University, quoting linguist, Dell Hymes, suggests, "Cultures possess communicative competencies for information sharing. The sender and receiver share rules of language, structure, form, topic, and event within a given culture" (*Delivering the Sermon* [Minneapolis: Fortress Press, 2008], 17). Communication is enhanced when the speaker and listener understand all the rules of engagement. Blue Note preaching is an experiential, dialogical performance. Like Bessie Smith, the preacher uses sound and musicality to persuade, paint, proclaim, and preach.

Blue Note preaching demands the preacher embody the Word. Stephen Webb refers to speech theory derived from Walter Ong, which is helpful to understand the sacred nature of speech, sound, and music: "Speech leaves no trace in space, and so it is a perfect medium for a God who does not want to be seen." (Webb, *The Divine Voice*, 33).

No other medium can carry the supernatural message with such power as sound.

Sound delivers something external but cannot be controlled. The written word can be copyrighted, and someone can say, "I own it." But once a word goes out, no one can own it or grab it. The only way you can recall it is through the reconstruction, with your imagination. Words can be copyrighted, visuals can be owned. Someone can keep them in his or her house, but not when it comes to speech, according to Ong and Webb. Once the sound has finished the act, only memory can reconstruct the evidence of the event. The act of producing speech and hearing what is produced is an intimate act. You can see light from a distance. Lighthouses can project light about eleven to fourteen miles; but with sound, the closer you are the better you can hear, because sound requires intimacy. No matter how big your speakers may be, no matter how deep the bass you may have in your car, sound still requires intimacy. The closer I am, the better I hear—the better I understand.

What is so interesting is that the Hebraic people share with us that God cannot be seen; God is encountered through sound and speech.

Look at this; God remixes physics in the creation of the world. In terms of physics, light travels faster than sound, but in order for God to create light, God has to speak that which is slower than light. Then light comes into being because of the sound. It is the sound that brings light into being. Once sound is released, then light is to be faster than sound. When Moses encounters God, it is not the visual of the burning bush, it is the sound of God he hears. Once he comprehends the intimacy of the sounds, then he has the visuals, God is here in the burning bush. It is in the Gospels. These disciples roll around with Jesus. You would think they would talk about, you know, he wore blue today, he wore red yesterday. But they don't talk about the visuals of Jesus—what he wore, what he looked like—no, they say, "What was his sound, what did he say?" The sound has power to set me free, because he is the Word that became flesh. It's the sound that empowers.

There is something called "auditory neurological brainstem response" that shows that sound has such power that it can change the way you view things. There are certain words that I can say that will release cortisol into your system, which causes stress, lowers your immune system, and makes you sick. You can say somebody's name, and cortisol will be released; it gives new meaning to the words, "You make me sick."

Scientists have discovered that there are other words that will release endorphins into your system. All you have to do is say that word and all of a sudden your immune system is lifted up. I believe it was a Duke University study that looked at certain words, and they were so confused because one word kept releasing more endorphins than another word. That word was *Jesus*! Every time they said *Jesus*, all of a sudden, even folk who didn't believe in Jesus, they felt better from hearing the word, *Jesus*! Because speech has power. Moses hears God. Jesus is the embodiment of God.

Literature and film are visual mediums, the canons of Western social construction. I am able to devalue you when I can canonize, concretize, and visualize. Sound refuses such easy description. Sound demands experience. Though it can be recorded, it cannot be captured. Music is recorded, but sound refuses to be owned. Who owns the sound of the sparrow? Who owns the sound of the wind? Who owns it but God? No one can have a patent that will go to the Supreme court to say, "I own that sound." We have patented DNA—everything—but we have yet in the corporate world to figure out how to patent sound. We haven't figured it out yet because sound speaks so powerfully of the Divine. It is forever lodged in the memories and minds of those who hear it. This is the power of preaching as an oral art of sound.

Blue Note preaching is oral and rooted in sound but also has a level of musicality to its construction. A theology is embedded in the chords of the Blue Note, and a theology is embedded in Blue Note preaching. This theology is transferred to the preacher. This is not just a cultural, oral performance; I contend that it is an embedded theology whose impact gives the form of preaching in a completely different way.

Jeremy Begbie, theologian and composer, in his brilliant book *Theology, Music, and Time*, speaks to the unique power of music to convey what words cannot. "Music can provide virtually nothing in the way of propositions or assertions" ([Cambridge, UK: Cambridge University Press, 2000], 11). Yet music does provide mood, color, and ideas in ways that words cannot.

Music is the only activity that engages the entire brain. Other activities, such as speech or memory, engage specific areas of the brain. Neuroscientist Oliver Sacks talks about a new music theory that deals with Alzheimer's patients. They've lost their memory, but if you play certain songs, all of a sudden all hemispheres of the brain are now working and the patients can recall things from forty to fifty years ago, just like that. The sound moves into them, and the sound begins to transform them (*Musicophilia : Tales of Music and the Brain* [Toronto: Vintage Canada, 2008]). Blue Note preaching recognizes this neurological fact. The call-and-response narrative found in the Black church is a part of a rich cultural and musical heritage of communication. Musical practice is socially and culturally embedded. It's not just people talking back to each other. There is theology going on. In the talking back is a new message that's being created. A canvas is being put up by the preacher that allows the people to join that moment.

The call and response from the church is connected to the African Griot tradition of West Africa. This way of preaching and communication was born against the backdrop of singing cicadas and humid air in the antebellum South. The preacher leads a dialogue; the congregation joins in to reshape this particular dialogue. It is the job of the preacher and the job of the congregation to join together and create a new musicality in the process.

I am reminded of a story that I heard from my father of a young man who is going to a homecoming in the western portion of Georgia. For those of you not familiar with homecoming in the South, it is a major deal. He was invited to preach, even though he'd had only one year of seminary. He was going to give the best homiletic presentation that they'd ever heard in their lives. Because he had one year of seminary, he was going to tell them all that he knew, what these country folk didn't know. Though he grew up in this church, he was going to throw in his Process Theology, his Liberation Theology. He was going to throw in a little bit of Niebuhr over here. He had some womanist ethics that he was going to throw in. He was going to throw in *everything* that he knew . . . in one sermon! He'd been working on this homiletical masterpiece for all of six weeks, knowing that he was going to present to this rural country group of people, so he could give them the greatest homiletical presentation that they had ever heard. Back in the day, they did not have air conditioning in the church.

He came and laid out all of his papers on the lectern and gave his preliminary remarks. All of the windows were open as he was about to give the greatest homiletical presentation that he'd ever given. All of the windows were open. It was hot. It was August. All of the windows were open. As he was about to speak, God had a sense of humor, and a breeze came through! His message went all over the church, and the only thing he could think to say was, "Ain't He alright? . . . Ain't He alright? . . . Ain't he, ain't He, ain't He," he sang. He said it for twenty minutes. You could hear the call and response of one mother in the church, "Help him, Lord!" Deacons put their heads down. But there was one woman, an elder, who was in the third row, and there she was just shouting, "I know He's alright! . . . He's alright! . . . He's good, He's alright. . . . He's good. . . . Say it, son, say it!" And everybody was looking at him, saying, "I hope he finishes soon!"

And he finished, and he stood in line, and he had to hear the messages and statements by people he grew up with, "Son you can come by and get some sweet potato pie if you want to. . . . Sorry what happened today, we praying *with you.*" One deacon just came and patted him on the back and kept going. Finally, he wanted to speak to that elder who had been shouting so much, who had been saying all that stuff; he was so confused. After everyone was gone, he went over to the elder and said, "Mother?"

She said, "Yes."

He said, "I saw that you were shouting."

She said, "Oh yes, I was shouting."

He said, "You did know that my message went everywhere, and all I said was ain't He alright."

She said, "Boy, that's *all* you said for twenty minutes
was ain't He alright!"

He said, "You did notice that I didn't have anything
to say?"

She said, "Oh yes, you didn't have *nothing* to say!"

He said, "Well can you please explain to me why you
shouted like it was the greatest message you ever heard?"

And she smiled at him and said, "Just because you
didn't do your job doesn't mean I'm not gonna do mine!"

There is a call and response that goes on in the midst
of the experience. There is a dialogue that happens in the
process. This active communication is part art, performance, and embodiment. The sermon is communal property. Christopher Small states, "Western composed music
is like a journey made by a composer who goes out, comes
back from 'out there' and tells us something, as best he can,
of what it was like" (quoted in Begbie, *Theology, Music, and
Time*, 183). Improvisation, dialogical music is a journey we
take together and discover something new.

The preaching journey with a Blue Note narrative
is a collective experience of the body. Blue Note preaching uses the musical format to reconstruct the work of
communication.

Blues lyrics use a typical AAB pattern of communication. Blues music uses a pentatonic scale. As I researched, I
didn't find anybody else who was talking about it at all. I was
looking at the pentatonic scale. That goes all the way back to
Mali. It is an African scale but is also used in European Folk
music, those pentatonic notes that we know as the Blues. I
discovered that, as the preacher comes to a close, all of a
sudden the cadence and musicality switch to a pentatonic

scale. So what the preacher is doing is saying one thing in terms of words but saying another thing in terms of sound. There is a double entendre that is happening in the midst of a close of a message. The words may say, "Jesus picked me up and turned me around," but the musicality of the sound is saying, "The Transatlantic slave trade could not destroy my connection to my past. I am shouting, not because of the sound; I'm shouting because I survived, and I'm still surviving." So don't mistake the shout as something that is just emotive. The shout also has theology behind it. I could stand up, and I could say Jesus is the ontological beginning that gives us existential understanding and moves us to eschatological hope, but it's easier just to say, "Thank you, Jesus!" It's the same thing. There is a double entendre that is happening in the midst of the communication. That is what goes on in the close of the message. Literally, you are reaching back to the Blues and recognizing that God is still moving in the midst. It is a theo-acoustic memory that is happening. We need to reclaim this, lift this up, and study this; that there is a speaking that goes all the way back to Mali. When the preacher begins to close—C. L. Franklin, Johnny Ray Youngblood, whoever it may be—you are actually closing with a rhythm that goes back almost a thousand years. There is a spiritual DNA in the call-and-response moment where two theologies are going on simultaneously. There is a beauty in this. There is also a theology of sound from the deep wellspring of culture. Evans Crawford and Thomas Troeger have documented this tradition well. Zora Neale Hurston and Lawrence Levine have also lifted this enduring tradition over and over again. Two modes of communication are going on when the preacher preaches a Theology of Words and a Theology of Sound.

August Wilson really helps me understand this idea so beautifully. One of my favorite plays is *The Piano Lesson* (1987), an absolutely beautiful tale that is the story of a gentleman by the name of Boy Willie and another character by the name of Berniece. They are brother and sister, and they have a piano that was given to them by their parents. This piano is unique. It comes from Mississippi. They live in Pittsburgh. This piano has carvings of Africa on one side and carvings of Europe on the other side. This piano was once owned by Mr. Sutter, who used to own the family. Boy Willie wants to sell the piano, because he no longer wants to be a prisoner of his past. Berniece says you cannot sell your past; you must hold on and come to grips with your past. But the unique aspect of the story is that there is a ghost in the story. A ghost you never see is Mr. Sutter, who is terrorizing Boy Willie; and at the close of the play, there's Boy Willie fighting with the ghost you do not see. The ghost is getting the best of Boy Willie. The only thing that Berniece can think to do is to sit down at the piano.

She begins to play the Blues. As she plays slowly, all of a sudden the fight begins to shift, because the sound of the Blues is now in the space, but still Sutter's ghost is getting the best of Boy Willie. Berniece begins to move from the Blues, going into almost a Holy Ghost Gospel shout. It begins to speed up, and as she speeds up in the playing, all of a sudden Boy Willie is able to fight and deal with Sutter because there is power in the sound. There is the power in that sound, and Boy Willie is able to throw Sutter's ghost out of the house. Now he is free from the haunts of his past, yet he still holds on to his past by not selling the piano.

That is the power of Blue Note preaching. Blue Note preaching is able to play a sound that does not cast the past away. Blue Note preaching allows a person to recognize pain but not fall into despair. Blue Note preaching uses a sound that has a double entendre. Blue Note preaching is so powerful that it can change the consciousness of an individual, and we give God thanks that there is a Blue Note and that there are people who are still preaching the Blue Note.

Click here for the original lecture video.

Chapter 3
HIP-HOP ENGAGEMENT WITH A POSTMODERN WORLD

The Blue Note preacher is the prophet of the modern age. She is the person staring in the darkness, finding God's image while others can see only despair. In chapter 1, we framed this Blue Note idea, and in the last chapter, we demonstrated the double entendre in Blue Note preaching through call and response. Now we want to look at the challenge of postmodern culture to preaching and methods inherent in Bebop, Hip-Hop, and even the Blues that allow us to speak to postmodern and post-Soul men and women.

A film came out a few years ago by James Cameron by the name of *Avatar*. It was one of the highest grossing films in history, poignantly displaying the clash of cultures and faith communities with modern society. For those who have not seen the film, it is the retelling of the old story of manifest destiny and colonialism. A planet far away from earth, rich with resources, is being colonized by humans to exploit the resources, yet the planet is inhabited by an agrarian, highly spiritual community of people known as the Na'vis. What is striking about the story is that the Na'vis, the traditional pastoral community, is completely computer-generated. The bringers of technology, human beings are live actors. The film puts the clash of culture, colonialism, the dangers of profit, and the destructive potential of technology on full display while using the latest form of technology to share a

parable, a simple parable about humanity's spiritual empti-
ness and the need to return to basic spiritual principles.

Avatar really raises the question about native and
immigrant culture. The clash that we are experiencing is
between digital natives and analog immigrants. "Digital
culture" can be defined, for our purposes, as anyone born
in the 1970s or later who has defined their entire life by
technological changes, a binary code of zeros and ones.
These are natural cultural distinctions, and this affects the
ways that we look at homiletics and preaching.

"Analog culture" uses wave technology. The pre-
dominant technical format since the turn of the century
has radically changed as a result of these binary codes. The
creation of mobile phones, personal computers, and GPS
occurred all throughout this extension of technology.

A simple test will tell if you are analog or digital. If
you ever owned a 78, a 45, or a 33, you are analog. If you
have ever called an audio device a "hi-fi," you are analog. If
you've ever purchased an 8-track tape, you're analog. If you
mailed a handwritten letter in the last two months, you are
straight up analog! If you looked up a number in a printed
phonebook—analog, analog!

Now, if you pay your bills online—digital. If losing
your cell phone means you would not know the number to
your own house, you are definitely digital! Losing your cell
phone is worse than losing your wallet—digital!

It is my contention that the major changes within
the world and faith community are not recent but part of a
glacial shift, a rapid technology shift. We are experiencing
a major shift that is really about digital and analog culture
clashing. You see, wave-analog technology is not mobile.
Digital technology is mobile. Digital and analog culture can
be further defined, then, as mobile and stationary.

I would even contend that there are digital biblical elements and analog biblical elements. If *analog* means that you have to come to the device, in digital culture the device comes to you and goes wherever you are. I would argue that there are digital elements in the story of the Ark of the Covenant moving across the plain of the desert. People moved where God said to move. That's a digital movement right there. But with the creation of the Temple, all of a sudden, people came to the Temple, and it had an analog element. People then had to come to worship, versus worship being wherever the people were.

Jesus then re-mixed and moved from this analog idea back to digital. Instead of you coming to a specific place, he said, "Wherever I am, also the spirit of God lies" (see John 12). Where does Christ worship? Christ worships outside. There is no better place to worship than looking at the canopy of Heaven. And so worship changes with this radical person by the name of Jesus, who begins to emphasize mobile culture all over again. All of a sudden he is saying things that can easily be replicated because of the focus on oral culture. "I've got to pass something on to you so you can pass it on to someone else." It is not text-based.

There is a major difference between the framing of Jesus and the framing of Paul. I would say Paul did have a mobile app, known as epistles, that he would pass on to the churches, but there is a difference between a rural framework and an urban framework. Jesus operated out of a rural framework (mobile and digital), and Paul operated out of an urban framework that was further framed by Roman culture (stationary and analog). This particular shift, from rural to urban, has affected preaching in the Christian tradition.

It really shifted in 1439, with the Guttenberg Bible. The Guttenberg Bible democratized faith to a degree, yes it did (digital). But at the same time, only certain people could own it (analog). Only those who were literate could tell you what was in the book. And that was the challenge of those kissed by Nature's sun, who came upon the shores of North America. Someone was telling them what the Bible means. That is the brilliance of Howard Thurman's grandmother, who said, "I like what Jesus says, but I got problems with that Paul guy. I don't read anything that Paul say; I wanna stick to what Jesus says!" (paraphrased from a story Thurman often told of her days as a slave). So the Guttenberg moment shifted the way that we view culture and preach today. There is now this analog and digital challenge.

DON'T DEIFY THE METHOD

Homiletics easily gets caught up in a particular methodology. People think there is only one way to preach, and that is not true. There are multiple ways in which someone can communicate, embody the Word of God, and pass that on to someone else. Don't ever idolize or deify a method.

Going back to the digital-test discussion, whether you place Amazing Grace on a 78, a 45, or a 33, an 8-track, a cassette tape, a CD, an MP3, on Spotify or Pandora, it is the same song; only the method of delivery is different. The problem is we have 8-track churches in an MP3 world, and we are wondering why we cannot reach a new generation. It is because we have deified the method.

Now let me see if I can break this down just a little bit. During the Beecher Lectures, I was accompanied by two musical friends. I had them both play "Amazing Grace," separately and then together. First, my friend Maggie played the hymn on her acoustic guitar. She moved us with a folk-sounding rendition of this familiar tune. Then my friend Wayne played a more funky version of the hymn on his electric guitar. It was just as moving. But finally, they played together, mixing both styles, and a totally new sensation was felt.

Different methodologies of playing, two different styles of playing, but they come together and there is something beautiful that happens. They are playing the same theme, the same song, but from two different perspectives. When homiletics, when preaching, recognizes that we don't deify a method—that what you bring to the table, God honors, God blesses, God anoints—all of a sudden, we can take acoustic, electrify it, and bring them together. We can take piano and Hammond, and they can play together. All of a sudden, you begin to create a Creole moment, where we bring the best of the elements from our own table and we create something new.

That is what is unique about the American project. We are always creating something new out of broken shards and pieces of people's lives. Something is created that is so unique and powerful. That is what I love about Blue Note preaching; it is translatable. It is the roux of American culture. You know that Jazz cannot swing without the Blues. Gospel cannot shout without the Blues. Soul cannot croon and Rock cannot roll, unless there is the Blues. Pop will never reach the charts without a Blues basis. Gospel, Jazz, R&B, and Hip-Hop all have particular Blues elements. Digital culture informs Blue Note homiletics.

JAZZ HARMONIES

So we have digital natives, and we have those who are analog immigrants. There is also a gap between a Guttenberg culture and a Google culture. You have these two elements fighting for dominance.

Digital culture and analog culture are dealing with this. Dwight Friesen, Leonard Sweet, and a computer scientist I studied, by the name of Matthew Dickerson, give us a glimpse of what digital faith has to offer the analog community.

The first thing that digital culture offers that also flows out of the Blues sensibility is what is known as an open source community. It reflects what I like about Google. I'm an Apple fan, but I really like the way Google flows. I just like the way they do things. "Open source" means you can create a program and others can add to that program. Take Google Maps as an example. Somebody said, "You know what? We need a map program, so I'm going to create a map program for me and my friends." Eventually, that person's program is added to the larger program. In other words, everyone is allowed to contribute. And the beautiful thing is, this idea of open source flows out of the Blues sensibility, which is really the Jazz motif understanding of how worship and preaching work together.

Let me break it down so that you understand what I am saying. The Jazz motif is something we can bring to preaching and also to worship where something unique happens. The power of Jazz is that Jazz does something that many styles of composition do not do. Jazz says, "Everybody has the right to solo. Even though you may have a different instrument coming from a different perspective, you have the right to solo." That's what I love about Jazz. The bass never tells the drum, "You gotta sound like me." The bass says, "I have my own unique perspective, and the sound that I bring to the table is something that contributes to the entire sound, and we work on this together." And so the drum gets to solo. What is unique is that, even in a Jazz band, it is the bringing together of African and European elements. You have a saxophone, which actually comes out of the marching-band element, as well as chamber music of the French tradition. Then you have a bass that is playing the baseline in polyrhythms that come out of the African tradition. All of these elements come together as they do, out of New Orleans, and each element has the right to solo.

The beautiful thing about Jazz is that Jazz taught democracy to America when America didn't even know what democracy was. This powerful dynamic is what also must happen in worship, because we do not operate with a Jazz motif. We are operating in a motif where the composer has already structured everything that will happen in worship. But you've got to have a Jazz moment every once in a while. Where the Spirit can show up, and all of a sudden somebody can solo in the midst of worship.

My two friends who played "Amazing Grace" didn't rehearse together, but the Spirit moved in such a way that worship happened as they brought their elements together. There is power when we do this together.

THE POST-SOUL GENERATION

The challenge is for those who are millennials. We don't want to talk with millennials or, as I like to say, the post-Soul generation. The post-Soul generation is defined in many different ways. If I were to use African American music as a marker to understand where we are culturally as a community and as a people, we are in a post-Soul moment.

This idea, this particular statement, was created by a writer by the name of Nelson George. He used to write for the *Village Voice*. *Post-Soul* means that we are no longer in the Soul era. Aretha Franklin, before she sang, "Respect," sang Soul music. Sam Cooke, before he sang, "You Send Me," sang with a Gospel group called the Highway QCs. That is Soul music. Marvin Gaye, before he said "What's Going On," was singing in a storefront Pentecostal church. That's Soul music. When you begin to talk about Kendrick Lamar, you begin to talk about Jay Z, you are now talking post-Soul. We are in a post-Soul moment. I believe Hip-Hop gives us a better understanding of how we are to engage in a postmodern era.

Hip-Hop did not begin ten years ago. It did not begin twenty or thirty years ago. It has now been more than forty years since a brother down in the South Bronx, DJ Kool Herc, did not have the money for guitars. He didn't have enough money for drums. He didn't have enough money for a saxophone, but his father had a bunch of James Brown records. He took those records and utilized his creativity and his imagination to find the break beat. He says to himself: "I don't have enough records, so I have to create a new song. So I find new rhythms, and in the process I take two turntables and keep the party rocking." So from 1971 until 1979, Hip-Hop was an underground phenomenon, operating mostly on the East Coast, where DJs used their unique musical skills to create something new. It was known specifically in adolescent communities on the East Coast.

But something happened in 1979 that changed everything for Hip-Hop. There was a group in Harlem, in an area called Sugar Hill, called the Sugar Hill Gang. Sugar Hill is the same place where Zora Neale Hurston used to spend her nights. The same place where Langston Hughes used to spend time. The same place where the Harlem Renaissance writers used to spend time. Out of Sugar Hill comes this group, the Sugar Hill Gang, who sing, "Rappers Delight." You know the song, "I said a hip, hop . . ." "Rappers Delight" becomes the first national engagement of this new form that borrows from the Griot tradition of Africa, of communicating meaning to people who are operating within a deindustrialized urban landscape. In 1979, it goes national.

In 1982, another group, Grand Master Flash and the Furious Five, begin to create a prophetic perspective of how to communicate in the world. Now remember that Hip-Hop is the first cultural creation that does not explicitly come out of the church. Blues is connected to spirituals. If you want to be able to sing Gospel, you have to know the Blues. Gospel is connected to the church. Obviously Jazz is connected to the church. Yes, R&B, Rhythm and Blues, Soul music are all deeply connected to the church. But Hip-Hop is standing outside of the church looking in the window because no one is raising questions about poverty and deindustrialized urban landscapes such as New York, L.A., and other places. Young people become the Griot to be able to speak prophetically when preachers said, "We will not speak."

HIP-HOP PREACHING

That is what happened. It is birthed out of that particular narrative. What does this have to say about preaching? Well, I believe that if you take the four pillars of Hip-Hop, you all of a sudden have a narrative and a framing for preaching. There are four pillars of Hip-Hop. For those who may not know it, there are Hip-Hop studies. Look at Tricia Rose, who's published an incredible book, *Black Noise: Rap*

Music and Black Culture in Contemporary America, which is probably the finest history of Hip-Hop culture that has been produced. It talks about the four elements of Hip-Hop: graffiti, break dancing, DJing, and rapping.

What in the world does graffiti have to do with preaching? Well, graffiti really is an aesthetic expression, the appropriation of space. It has been operating in the church for quite some time, where it is called stained glass. That which was street has been elevated to art that we now say is sacred. That which could not be shown because Caesar was considered to be the Son of God now has been elevated to that which is considered to be sacred. So it was the artistic expression of the appropriation of space because space also preaches, which means that preachers must be cognizant of the space in which they preach.

The pillar of aesthetic also speaks to break dancing. This is about movement and kinetic energy, the idea that the utilization of one's body can express things that words cannot. If you want God to completely use you—God, as we discussed earlier, is embodiment—let your preaching be embodied, however that may be.

The third element of Hip-Hop is the DJ. You might ask, "Do we now replace the organ with the DJ?" I am not necessarily saying that, but I am saying we must consider the appropriation of technology in worship. There was a time when there were no pipe organs in the church. Their arrival was the appropriation of technology. Now we have an opportunity to appropriate technology once again. We can utilize technology to communicate a message that is, again, another pillar of Hip-Hop.

Finally, rapping, which is just oral dexterity, rhetorical proficiency . . . how you spit your lyrics when you communicate.

These are the particular pillars that give us a framework for how we are to engage liturgically and how we are to engage homiletically; the embodiment, the space, the appropriation, and the rhetorical proficiency of the person who is communicating. To communicate so that people understand.

Post-Soul preaching and designs, sermons that have a post-Soul liturgy, and Blue Note preaching make demands of post-Soul culture to create a *360* liturgical narrative. What is this *360* thing? It means that everybody learns differently. There are some people in your congregation, as my friend, D. Daryl Griffin says, who are head folk. They want something that is broken down in a very didactic way. Then there are some heart folk; you got to tell some stories. Then there are some gut folk. They want you to move from the page. But these people are all in the same sanctuary, which means you have to be a student of the people in your sanctuary. You must understand, so you cannot be married to one way of communication, because you may not reach them with that form of communication. Or you may have to bring someone in who communicates in a different way.

That is the power of Blue Note sensibilities but also the utilization of what I call the Jazz Methodology of preparation. Jazz is structured around the Blues. Gospel is structured around the Blues. Blues is birthed from spirituals and work songs and call-and-response narrative in the church. This methodology builds new music around the theme of bending notes, flatting the fifth, and returning to the theme on an appropriate beat. This form of preaching, Jazz methodology, is dangerous. The Blue Note preacher is prepared to take a risk. Jazz musicians and musicians who dare to use an improvisational narrative take a risk every time. The Blue Note preacher is prepared and takes a risk. Jazz is dangerous because it dares to create a new composition while playing the old. Right in front of the people, something new is created. The musician dares to look behind a new door and find a gift God has left right behind the door. We call it improvisation, call and response, the Holy Spirit. The Holy Spirit is in charge of liturgical preparation and homiletical proclamation. We are called to prepare diligently. But since Blue Note preaching demands the embodiment of an experiential outcome, we must be open to risk leaving what we have prepared. It means that we must be sensitive to the moment when we must make a shift, because we may miss an opportunity to communicate clearly to someone who needs to hear that which has been given to us.

I had an experience with this in a very unique and powerful way. I was doing a particular sermon series, and in one sermon I was talking about David. Preachers talk about David all of the time. He is one of the favorite people we love to talk about. It was placed on my spirit to talk about David from a different perspective, in first person, number one. Then, number two, to talk about David as a failure as a father. Talk about how we love to lift him up as a great political leader; but what would David say to men in Chicago? What would he say to those on the South Side? That he gave his entire life for the kingdom, and he destroyed his family? What would he say, that Absalom and Amnon actually learned their behavior from him? What would he say, that his daughter never talked to him, and he never spoke up for Tamar? I prepared for weeks and weeks. I had a script together, but it could never be read exactly as it was written. It was very clear to me that I must embody David. I must invite David. I must know the smell of the kingdom. I must understand his thoughts. I must become David. I remember preaching that day. It was a strange experience and in one moment my eyes welled up in tears as David was talking about his child and his failures. David was sharing from his childhood that his daddy didn't think he could be anointed to be king and how that continues to walk with him. All through the entire message, I allowed David to speak. After that improvisational moment of allowing David to speak, a twelve-year-old young man came up to me and said, "David, you talked about my family." He didn't refer to me as Pastor Moss or Rev. O, but as David. Then a twenty-year-old man came over and said, "Thank you for explaining what happened in my house." The embodiment, the embodiment—that which God has place before us. The improvisational moment requires being sensitive to what is happening at moment. That is what God has called us to do.

One of the greatest improvisational Blue Note moments in American history was Martin Luther King's "I Have a Dream" speech. He had prepared very well. We love that close! But he did not prepare that close. He stood on the mall in Washington D.C. and was sensitive to that moment. In that particular moment, he stood on the mall and said, "I have a dream that one day even the state of Mississippi, a state sweltering with the heat of injustice, sweltering with the heat of oppression, will be transformed into an oasis of freedom and justice" (www.archives.gov/press /exhibits/dream-speech.pdf, 5–6). He then continued with that refrain that we so deeply love, "I have a dream." But it was a remix, because he heard a sister by the name of Dr. Prathia Hall-Wynn use that narrative, and in the midst of that particular moment, he reappropriated that remix. So Dr. King was remixing back and forth as he was speaking at that time, and presented that to the world, and now it echoes in the consciousness of the American project. All from an improvisational moment, Jazz methodology. Absolutely brilliant!

Jesus preaches with these Jazz elements. He is always being confronted, and then there are those improvisational moments, whether it is someone touching the hem of a garment or meeting a man with many demons.

Improvisation is not an art exclusive to Jazz, Blues, or African-inspired North American traditions. If we look even at the kinetic brilliance of basketball and soccer, we get an idea of how improvisational excellence is developed. Any type of transition game, such as basketball, demands skill and knowledge of the game. One must understand the dynamics and ebb and flow of the game; yet it is a game open to improvisation and acts of imagination that other sports can only dream of.

My son, Elijah, he's something else! This gentleman has heart! He stands so tall at 5'2". But you would think he's 6'10". Talks stuff to everybody. Looking up at one of his mentors, Julian Gaines, who is 6'6", he says, "I can take you!" He's got heart! I share my knowledge and love of the game with him. We spend time practicing. He spends time practicing his solo: dribble left, dribble right, right, left, behind the back, no look pass, jump shot, fake, and rebound. He always studies the greats of the game. So he knows about Magic, LeBron, Michael, Maya Moore, Larry Byrd, Bill Russell, Jason Williams, Chris Paul, Kyrie Irving, and Jason Kidd. The list goes on and on. He fails most of the time as he's practicing these particular moments, because he never knows if he'll ever have an opportunity to use them in a game. He is not stuck on textbook x's and o's. He is working his craft like a Jazz musician and a Blue Note preacher. He is preparing for his solo that may never come.

But the beauty is, he's preparing for the solo. He believes that, "I'm going to have the opportunity, even though every day in the backyard I fail. But if I triumph one time, one time is good enough for me, so I will work this particular piece!" He has me out there; I have a broom that I hold up so that he can shoot over somebody who is over 7' tall. He has heart.

His methodology is how preaching should be prepared. You need to prepare. You need to study the greats. You need to look at them, and you will fail most of the time in your preparation. But that one time that God and the Spirit move in such a way that puts things together all of a sudden—boom, three points, you got it! God will do that every once in a while. It is in the failure during the preparation that you begin to develop and become the preacher God wants you to be. You become great in your failures, over and over and over and over. Flunk will visit the pulpit with you and hang out and spend time talking to you, telling you, "You need to leave the pulpit." But keep working your solo. Just as it is in basketball, it is the same in soccer. Pele's beautiful scissor kick is not something you learn from your coach. You learn that as you use your imagination and you're working day to day as a child.

The Jazz method of Blue Note preaching challenges us to do the work. We are called to study the craft, develop our own voices, if we are to improve our homiletical ability. We must study those out of our tradition. However, if all you study are people in your own denomination, ethnic background, gender, sexual orientation, racial classification, or educational pedigree, you will limit your gifts. You have to study beyond that with which you are comfortable. It is not that you are willing to become just like that person, but you should learn those particular gifts and study.

My son taught me that. He was studying Kareem Abdul-Jabbar. He wasn't alive when Kareem was playing, but he studied Kareem and Bill Russell because he wants to know the greats. He wants to understand the greats. Can you imagine someone saying, "I refuse to listen to and study Stevie Wonder because he plays music by ear?" Can you imagine someone saying, "I will not study Woody Guthrie because he did not graduate from college?" Can you imagine someone saying, "I will not study James Baldwin because he was gay?" Can you imagine someone saying, "I will not study Toni Morrison because she does not have a PhD in literature?"

Let me give you an example of the brilliance of a person, a brilliant person who helps us understand the Blues and Jazz aesthetic of study and preparation. This particular person who lets us understand study and preparation is a brother by the name of James Brown. I know some might ask, "How does James Brown end up in this book?" I'm about to break it down so you'll understand. James Brown is the best example of congregational exegesis. James Brown, the godfather of Soul, is the greatest exegetical practitioner of organic kinetic sensibilities. In other words, James Brown knows how to teach people how to get "funky" even when they don't know what getting "funky" is all about!

James Brown was raised in Augusta, Georgia, and influenced by the pentatonic rhythms of the United House of Prayer for All People, founded by Marcelino Manuel da Graça, better known as Daddy Grace. This music was a form of Blues influenced by West African tonal traditions. Pentatonic music of Africa and Eastern Europe clap on the upbeat. James Brown recognized the difficulty for many Americans, who were unfamiliar with pentatonic traditions, to dance to music designed on the upbeat. He decided to change the structure from the upbeat to the downbeat, giving wider access to mainstream America. His exegesis of audience gave wider appeal to his music. He was still funky, but he changed when the beat would begin, allowing a new wave of disciples to be trained in the art of Rhythm and Blues. This simple idea expresses the need for the preacher to exegete your context, congregation, and your space. If your goal is to communicate, why wouldn't you want to know where the people are? Stop asking them to climb with you. Get out of the pulpit and be with them. But be yourself.

When I prepared to give the Beecher Lectures at Yale, someone told me, "Otis, you talk fast, and you move around a lot. You need to just stand there and read very quietly."

I said, "I can't do that. That wouldn't be me!" There is nothing more deadly in preaching than when you are inauthentic. Be who you are. No one can be a better you than you. There's nothing wrong with studying other people, but learn to find your voice. It takes time to find your voice. I am still trying to find my voice. We do it over time. Howard Thurman said, "God places a crown over our heads, which for the rest of our lives we keep trying to grow tall enough to wear" (*Jesus and the Disinherited* [Boston: Beacon Press, 1996], 106 paraphrased). We will spend a lifetime trying to find our voice.

I believe that James Brown teaches us how to read scripture using Jazz methodology. Learn how to read it out loud. Read it with different dynamics, pauses, and inflections. Close your eyes, imagine the people, sounds, and colors. Imagine these things and begin to paint pictures in your head. Close your eyes and imagine the moment you are to preach, envision yourself in the act of what God is doing with you. God never arrives because of us. God arrives in spite of us. We are the worst instruments to communicate the Holy. It is Gardener Taylor in his 1975–76 Beecher Lecture who said, "The foliage of Connecticut is better equipped to communicate the Gospel than the voice of someone who is human." But yet, God trusts us. It would be better for a sunrise to talk about the beauty of God than myself or anyone reading this book. It would be better for a tree to communicate the beauty of God than us, but God trusts us. Taylor says that is the foolishness of preaching; that God would use somebody who does not have the capacity to fully communicate and is so deeply broken. But it is in these moments, when you take that which you have and you give it to God—it is when you give it to God—God will do something unique and new in the process.

In closing, I will tell you this story. Monica and I love going to New Orleans. We love the "NOLA." We are fans of New Orleans and everything about New Orleans. We were walking along the streets in the French Quarter, and there was a gentleman painting in this store. We decided to go into the store. He was like the people of New Orleans, who love to talk to you and always have a story. So as we looked at his paintings—which were beautiful, wonderful—we asked about the cost of some of them. He had these paintings of different people and whatnot. He said, "I can paint anything that you want." I asked, how much are these over here? He said those are twenty dollars. I said that's a good price for this large canvas. How much are these over here? He said, "Oh, those are fifteen hundred dollars." Now these are by the same artist. Why are these so much more than those over there? He said, "Oh, these I painted. The ones over there God designed."

I said, "Please explain that to me!"

He said, "You have to understand, I did the work on these paintings right here, but God gave me an assignment that I would then paint something and while the paint was fresh, God would tell me to take the painting, while it was fresh and still wet, take it out into a storm and leave it out in the storm. When the storm beats on the canvas, something unique will be created in the process."

So take that which you have into the storm. Do not put before the people just who you are. Take your gifts and give them to God. Let God utilize those gifts, and God will beat upon the canvas of your spirit and create something new that has never been created before. Take your spirit and your soul into the storm, and God will create a Blue Note perspective that you have never seen in your life. May God bless you and may God keep you.

Click here for the original lecture video.

Sermon 1

LOVING YOU IS KILLING ME

Judges 16

(This sermon was preached at Trinity United Church of Christ on August 24, 2014, as part of a series of sermons on scandals in the Bible.)

I want to read from the NIV version and the OM3 (the Otis Moss III) translation of this sacred text beginning with verse 1. The NIV version, verses 1–21, goes this way:

> One day Samson went to Gaza, where he saw a prostitute. He went in to spend the night with her. The people of Gaza were told "Samson is here!" So they surrounded the place and lay in wait for him all night at the city gate.
> They made no move during the night, saying, "At dawn we'll kill him."
> But Samson lay there only until the middle of the night. Then he got up and took hold of the doors of the city gate, together with the two posts, tore them loose, bar and all. He lifted them to his shoulders and carried them to the top of the hill that faces Hebron.
> Some time later he fell in love with a woman in the valley of Sorek whose name was Delilah. The rulers of the Philistines went to her and said, "See if you can lure him into showing you the secret of his great

66

strength and how we can overpower him so that we may tie him up and subdue him. Each one of us will give you eleven hundred shekels of silver.

So Delilah said to Samson, "Tell me the secret of your great strength and how you can be tied up and subdued."

Samson answered her, "If anyone ties me with seven fresh bowstrings that have not been dried, I'll be weak as any other man." Then the rulers of the Philistines brought her seven fresh bowstrings that had not been dried, and she tied him with them. With men hidden in the room, she called to him, "Samson, the Philistines are upon you!" But he snapped the bowstrings as easily as a piece of string snaps when it comes close to a flame. So the secret of his strength was not discovered.

Then Delilah said to Samson, "You have made a fool of me; you lied to me. Come now, tell me how you can be tied."

He said, "If anyone ties me securely with new ropes that have never been used, I'll become as weak as any other man."

So Delilah took new ropes and tied him with them. Then, with men hidden in the room, she called to him, "Samson, the Philistines are upon you!" But he snapped the ropes off his arms as if they were threads.

Delilah then said to Samson, "All this time you have been making a fool of me, baby, and lying to me. Tell me how you can be tied."

He replied, "If you weave the seven braids of my head into the fabric on the loom and tighten it with the pin, I'll be as weak as any other man." So while he was sleeping, Delilah took the seven braids out of his head, wove them into the fabric, and tightened it with the pin

Again she called to him, "Samson, the Philistines are upon you!" He awoke from his sleep and pulled up the pin and the loom, with the fabric.

Then she said to him, "How can you say 'I love you' when you won't confide in me? This is the third time you have made a fool of me and haven't told me the secret of your great strength." With such nagging, she prodded him day after day until he was sick to death of it.

So he told her everything. "No razor has ever been used on my head," he said, "because I have been a Nazarite dedicated to God from my mother's womb. If my head were shaved, my strength would leave me, and I would become as weak as any other man."

When Delilah saw that he had told her everything, she sent word to the rulers of the Philistines, "Come back once more; he has told me everything." So the rulers of the Philistines returned with silver in their hands. After putting him to sleep on her lap, she called for someone to shave off the seven braids of his hair, and so began to subdue him. And his strength left him.

Then she called, "Samson, the Philistines are upon you!"

He awoke from his sleep and thought, "I'll go out as before and shake myself free." But he did not know that the LORD had left him.

Then the Philistines seized him, gouged out his eyes and took him down to Gaza. Binding him with bronze shackles, they set him to grinding grain in the prison. But the hair on his head began to grow again after it had been shaved.

Now moving down to verses 26–30:

Samson said to the servant who held his hand, "Put me where I can feel the pillars that support the temple, so that I may lean against them." Now the temple was crowded with men and women; all the rulers of the Philistines were there, and on the roof were about three thousand men and women watching Samson perform. Then Samson prayed to the LORD, "Sovereign LORD, remember me. Please, God, strengthen me just once more, and let me with one blow get revenge on the Philistines for my two eyes." Then Samson reached toward the two central pillars on which the temple stood. Bracing himself against them, his right hand on the one and his left hand on the other, Samson said, "Let me die with the Philistines!" Then he pushed with all his might, and down came the temple on the rulers and all the people in it. Thus he killed many more when he died than while he lived."

We're in a series on scandals, the scandals of the Bible, and today we want to deal with the subject of this story of Samson with the heading of: "Loving You Is Killing Me."

Loving you is killing me. Turn to your neighbor at this time, look at your neighbor, smile at your neighbor, and say, "Neighbor, oh neighbor, I want you to know, you need to be careful who you love." Then find another neighbor, maybe the same one, and say "Neighbor, oh neighbor. The person you hook up with can blind you." Amen.

Loving you is killing me. Beloved, an anointing does not exempt you from foolish decisions and stupid actions.

There is a belief that because you are called, have accepted Christ, and are filled with the Holy Ghost that you are somehow insulated from the human proclivity to search out unhealthy action and hook up with dysfunctional people. If we search . . . if we search the DVR of our memory, we see that the people who made some of the worst relationship decisions were not unchurched secular people who never had an encounter with God, but people who claimed to know Christ.

Can I just be real today with you all? Some of our greatest relationship nightmares were not standing in the bar, hanging in the club, but sitting in the pew. I'm reminded of the quotation that Deacon Lawrence Miles stated, and blessed me, and I will never forget. He said, "God saved my soul, but he is still working on my character."

Salvation is immediate; sanctification is progressive. What this statement is saying is that salvation is the saving action of God to claim the essence of who we are, but sanctification is the progressive, the progressive action of the Holy Spirit upon my heart and my character. In other words, God is working on me, though God has saved me, and I'm compelled to share with you what God has placed on my heart about the scandals of the Bible. Many times we are in a drama, but we don't realize that we are the writers of the drama, and we want to blame the guest star in our drama for causing the drama that we wrote in the first place.

This is a practical message. It will not make you shout, but it is designed to save someone's life. Truth be told, we fail, we fail miserably as a community, in and around relationships. We live in a myth or a concept. We seek a fantasy. We desire a dream. We are never educated on the reality of building a relationship.

We want happy, stress-free romance-induced fantasies, because we've been watching too much *Grey's Anatomy* or Love Jones, or you were reading *Fifty Shades of Grey*, or whatever you may be reading. Or maybe you are too worried about what Olivia Pope and Fitz are doing on *Scandal*.

Even in the canon of the culture of America, we believe in life, liberty, and the pursuit of happiness. When you watch a fable, a fairy tale, at the end—when the prince and the princess get together—it says, and they lived . . .

Yes, happily ever after.

We like that word *happy*, but good relationships are not based on the happy quotient. In the words preached by Dr. Freddie Haynes, "Happiness deals with what's happening in your life." Relationships are hard. Relationships are hard, relationships are hard, relationships are hard. There's no way around it, it's difficult. You're going to deal with challenges, no matter what, but good relationships must be worked on, fought for, and taught.

I am reminded of the story of Reverend Tony Campolo. I heard him tell about a gentleman who was taking care of his wife who had Alzheimer's, and everyone was saying, "Put her in a home, she does not remember you, she doesn't know who you are, she does not remember you." But this gentleman said something that pushed everybody back and blessed everyone. He said, "She does not remember me, but I remember her." He said, "I refuse to do that, because of all that she has done in my life. I can at least take care of her as she pitches her tent closer to the River Jordan." This man, according to Campolo, was probably not happy, but he had built a good relationship. We have

a difficulty dealing with this idea, because we're trying to
always protect our hearts and our spirits, and we even give
such poor advice to our children and our extended families around relationships. You'll ask your parents or your
friends or your mentors, "How do you know when you are
in love?" And the answer will be . . . ?

Yes, "You'll know."

"You'll know." That's terrible advice to give to
somebody!

The problem is that we have shifted as a culture from
courting to dating. There is a major difference between
courting and dating. *Dating*—let me break it down to you
all—is a lie. When you date somebody, all you're trying to
do is share with that person what you think they want to
hear from you; and that person is trying to share with you
what they think you want to hear. You're not telling all your
crazy stuff, all the mess that's gone on in your life, because
you want to connect with that individual. But courting,
you see, works differently. Those who are from the South
remember how courting operated.

Courting is not about two people connecting. It
is about an entire community trying to discover whether
those two people have the same value system. If you wanted
to court a person, especially in the South, you see, you had
to meet the parents first. And the question was, not where
you work, but who are your people, because this has to do
with whether you have the same value system.

They wouldn't even let you into the house. You
couldn't cross the threshold, you had to spend time on the
front porch, and the window had to be open as you were
talking so someone else could listen in; because they under-
stood that when you are all in love you can't make good
decisions. You need to have somebody in your life who's

able to examine things that you can't see. Many people got into trouble in relationships who started out dating, lying in the process. Later, if they got together, they asked, "Where did all of this stuff come from?" because they were dating and not courting and didn't have somebody who had they best interests at heart to be able to say, "You don't need to bother with this person in the first place, because I've observed how he treats his mamma." "I've observed how she treats everybody else, and now I see that this is not somebody that you need to be connected with."

Samson, this anointed and appointed brother by God, was birthed and ordained. An angel whispered into the hearts of his parents that "You shall raise a boy who is a Nazarite. He will be set apart for God. He will know about the word of God." Obviously, his parents taught him scripture and brought him to the temple, but they did not teach him about love.

Samson was a strong man; he could kill a lion with his bare hands, ah, he was blessed with physical prowess and beauty. When he came into a room, the sisters would swoon. He was a dark chocolate brother, looked like a cross between Idris Elba and Boris Kodjoe. He had long dreadlocks, was doing his thing. Every time he came into a room, the sisters would fall out and start fanning themselves, because here comes Samson.

But Samson, though he was set apart as a Nazarite, though he was one that was committed unto God, Samson had a proclivity. He always hooked up with women below his level. If you read from chapters 14 through 16, you will notice something strange about Samson. His first wife was a Philistine; he had to "go down" to Timnah to find his wife. Then it says here in chapter 16 that he goes down to Gaza to be with a prostitute; then he goes down into a valley—in the Valley of Sorek—to be with Delilah. Every time he has to hook up with somebody, he has to "go down," he has to go below his level. You see I believe that birds should fly with birds, cats should walk with cats, dogs should run with dogs, and children of God should run with children of God.

The first thing you should ask somebody before you make a connection with them is not where do you work, or where do you live. You need to ask, "Do you know Jesus?" That's the first question that I have to ask. As a matter of fact, if you ever go to the bank, they have all these different drawers for different denominations; they have a one-dollar drawer, a five-dollar drawer, they've got a ten-dollar and a twenty-dollar drawer and so on and so on, but I've never seen a twenty-dollar bill trying to jump into the one-dollar drawer. There's a reason they try to separate values. The one dollar stay with the one dollars. The five dollars stay with the five dollars, the tens stay with the ten, and the twenty with the twenty. The question to Samson is, why are you trying to hook up with a dollar person when God has given you higher value? You need to be connected with somebody of the same value. Delilah, whose name means "flirtatious," she's fine with me. I like Delilah because there's no lying in Delilah. Delilah is straight up.

She tells you exactly what she wants. "I think ye fine, but I want you to understand, I'm not in this for the long haul, you see. I think you good looking and all that, but I want you to understand, my value system is different from yours, and no matter how much you pray, no matter how much you hang out with me, I'm not converting to be an Israelite. I'm gonna always be a Philistine."

There are those of us who are always praying that the Philistine we hooked up with will become an Israelite. But they ain't changing from the Philistine that they've been.

They were a Philistine when you met 'em; they're going to be a Philistine while you with 'em; they're going to be a Philistine after you leave 'em; they're always going to be a Philistine. They're not making a shift, because they like their value system. So Samson hooks up with people who are below his level, but here is something that you need to see; it says in the text that he went into the Valley of Sorek, and he fell in love with Delilah. Never hook up with someone who doesn't love you.

If you read the scripture, Samson loved Delilah. You will not find it anywhere in the Bible where Delilah loves Samson, but Samson was all in love with Delilah. Part of our challenge is that when we fall in love, we end up having these strange fantasies and even—how should I put it—we even start singing these old crazy songs too, you know, just . . . just crazy songs don't make no kind of sense.

Now for the old school folk, you remember *Dreamgirls* the play that had Jennifer Holliday; for new school, you remember *Dreamgirls* the movie that had Jennifer Hudson. Each character—in the play and in the movie—they both sang the same song, and there's a line in there that makes no sense.

It says, "You gonna love me." No, you're not. It's not going to happen. I'm sorry. You need to stop singing that song. You are not going to make anybody love you who does not want to love you. That's why God invented something great on Facebook called "unfriend." There are some people we need to unfriend and some people we need to unfollow.

If you are always in love with people who are not in love with you, they will manipulate your love for them. You say, "Well, well can we make this permanent, can we make a commitment, you know, get a commitment together? We've been together for a while."

And then the person will say, "You know what I'm saying, you know, we been together long enough, you know what I'm saying, there ain't no book can tell us that I love you, you know what I'm saying? This book been messed over by people, this the white man's book. I love you. We ain't need that. We don't need to walk down the aisle. We share fifty percent of everything as we living in your mamma's basement, don't you understand this? I got you, I got you."

People will manipulate you when you love them and they do not love you. Never hook up with someone who you say you love, but who doesn't love you.

Here's the other thing, now I gotta talk to Samson. Samson, let me just talk to Samson. Samson, you fell in love with Delilah; you say you love Delilah, "I love me some Delilah." Yeah, yeah, yeah, "You love you some Delilah"; you love Delilah, but if you're so in love with Delilah, why do you keep lying to her? It's right here in the Bible; he fell in love with Delilah, and Delilah says, "Baby, tell me the secret of your great strength."

And Samson says, "Well, if you get seven fresh bowstrings that have never been dried, I'll be as weak as any other man."

Then she ties him up while he's asleep. At 3:00 a.m., brothers come from out of the closet, from behind the couch. Now it seems to me that, at 3:00 a.m., when all of a sudden some other folks show up at the house, you would raise a few questions. But he breaks the bowstrings, beats up the brothers, kicks them out, and goes back to Delilah's house, and he's with Delilah again.

And Delilah gets her Delilah talk going, "Baby, you making a fool of me, just tell me," as she's rubbing his bicep, "What's the secret of your great strength?"

He says, "Well, if you get some rope ain't nobody ever used, and tie me up, Sweetie, I'll be as weak as any other man."

"Oh, okay, go to sleep." And 3:00 a.m. brothers come from out of everywhere. He has to beat them down again. Three times he does this, and Delilah keeps on saying, then she manipulates his love. "How can you say you love me, and you won't let me tie you up and subdue you and know the secret of your great strength?" She manipulated his love. Samson wanted this fantasy. He wanted this idea of being in love; and you gotta be careful who you claim to love, especially if they don't love you. In my mind, I'm thinking, and it's not in the text, but it's in my sanctified imagination, the question from Samson to Delilah should have been, "So who are all these brothers that keep showing up at the house?"

You know, "They my play cousins." You know, "We been knowing each other since we were little." And if you, if you got somebody, and people keep showing up at the house in places they shouldn't be, texting things they should not text, sending posts they should not send, no SnapChat and shouldn't be on it—hmm—that raises some questions about the relationship. And the other thing that I would raise to Samson is, "Why are you attracted to people who are below your level? What is the attraction? Delilah doesn't share your values. There's something there. You keep going to people that you know will hurt you."

And the other thing is simply this, if you forget everything else I say, remember this: protect your secret. It's your secret. Now if you share the secret with everybody, it ain't a secret. It's called public knowledge. One must protect one's secret, because it's your secret. There are people who simply want to be with you to know your secret so they can tell everybody else, "I know that person's secret." Sharing your secret with the wrong person can lead to blindness. Samson shared his secret with Delilah, and eventually she nagged him and put him to sleep on her lap. They cut his hair, and he thought that he was going to be just like every other time, "I will go, and I will throw them out of the room," but the Lord had left him.

Sharing your secret with the wrong person leads to blindness. That's pretty much what I wanted to share, but there's some good news here. You can be in the wrong relationship. You can mess up over and over again, but God can redeem you from the wrong relationship. See, here's the simple thing that you need to know. Samson never hooked up with Delilah again. Even though they threw him in prison, he was not running around saying, "Delilah, please come visit me." He was not trying to be a pen-pal with her. He was in the prison, thinking about the mistake that he had made by running after somebody who was below his level.

He did not raise the question, do you know Yahweh, do you know Jehovah, are you on the same level with me? He never hooked up with Delilah again.

My friend Howard John Wesley tells the story about when his children were small, and they were traveling. They were in an airport, and his youngest child had to go to the restroom. So he put him in the stall and told him what he needed to do. The boy soon started yelling, saying, "Daddy, Daddy, I need help!"

And he asked, "What's wrong?"

The boy said, "There's no handle to flush the mess here, Daddy, there's no handle to flush the mess."

And his father had to help him out. He said, "Son, if you want to get rid of the mess you've got—this is an automatic commode—you've got to learn how to turn and walk away." And if you want to flush some people out of your life, one of the things that you gotta learn how to do is turn and walk away.

And so Samson never hooked up with Delilah again. But here is the good news, right here. They cut Samson's hair, but while he was in prison, his hair started to grow back. His hair started to grow again. In other words, they cut his hair, but he still had his roots. I can fall sometimes, but if I still have my roots then "Greater is he that is within me than he that is in the world" (see 1 John 4:4). I've got my roots. If you know your roots, then no weapon formed against you shall prosper. That's your root. You need to have your roots. In modern times, if you have no hair on Sunday, technology will allow you to have hair on Monday. Modern technology allows you to do this. It's usually called a weave. There's nothing wrong with it. I ain't talking about that, I'm talking about the fact that some have spiritual weaves, and when they join church on Sunday they think they're ready to preach on Monday. You see it takes time to develop in the Lord, and it takes a moment to grow to have a relationship with God. You've got to spend some time with God to grow and develop.

There was a gentleman who joined here on one Sunday, and then the next week he had a collar and said that he had been called by God. He didn't need to go to seminary because God had given him everything. He had joined last week, and God had given him everything that he needed to know in the Bible, and he was ready to be on the staff here at Trinity United Church of Christ. The only thing that I could say to him was, "Brother, it's a spiritual weave. All I'm saying is that what you have, you have not allowed it to grow in you. You've got to grow and develop and go through some things in order for you to develop spiritually." But what I love about Samson is that you will notice something when he is in prison. It says that he prayed to the Lord.

Now if you read all of Samson's story, you will notice that Samson never prayed until he was in prison. He lost his eyes, and he lost his strength. Then all of a sudden he's praying to God. Sometimes God has to remove some things so that you will begin to consult God in reference to your decisions. And sometimes you need to thank God that God removed some things from your life, because you learned how to pray and get on your knees and begin to talk to God, because you were not talking to God in the first place. Sometimes your adversity will put you on your knees, your trouble will put you on your knees, your problems will put you on your knees. There are moments when you will get on your knees because you've been through some things.

Samson is honest. He says, "I messed up, Lord, just remember me. I lost my strength, you left me. I hooked up with the wrong people, but just give me enough strength so that I may defeat your enemies, my enemies." And so Samson, who could not see, said to the servant, "Just put me near one of the pillars." And they brought Samson out just to laugh at him. Ah, but Samson said, "Let me be near a pillar," and he put one hand on one pillar and another hand on another pillar. And he just prayed to the Lord, "Just give me strength, just one more time. Give me strength one more time to be able to take out those who took out my eyes." And Samson pushed on the pillars and brought down the temple. But scripture says this, "He killed more in his death than he did in his life." In other words, he did more after he messed up than before he messed up, and that's what I love about God. God can do more with you after you mess up.

God did more with Abraham after he messed up with Sarah. God did more with Jacob after he stole the birthright of his brother. God did more with Moses after he killed an Egyptian. God did more with Job after he lost his family. God did more with David after he committed adultery. God did more with Peter after he denied Jesus. God did more with Paul after he persecuted those who followed Christ. But let me tell you, God did more with Jesus after he died on Calvary than before he died on Calvary, because when he died, then on Sunday morning, he got up with all power and he saved you and he saved me. And what that means is that we serve a God who will give you a second chance.

Oh, I'm sorry, not a second chance, a third chance; no, a fourth chance; no, a fifth chance; number six, seven, eight, nine, ten, eleven, twelve, thirteen, fourteen, fifteen, sixteen, seventeen. Just shout when I get to your number eighteen, nineteen; any twentys in the house? Twenty-one, twenty-two, twenty-three, any twenty-fours in the house? Twenty-five, twenty-six, twenty-seven? . . . God will keep blessing you over and over and over and over. If God has given you more than one more chance, if God has given you more than two chances, you need to say "Thank you that you gave me another chance." "Thank you that you blessed me one more day." "Thank you that you woke me up this morning." You're a second-chance God, you're a third-chance God. You're a fourth-chance God.

Sermon 2

GAME OF THRONES

(This sermon was preached at Trinity United Church of Christ as a first-person sermon that attempts to embody the blues. I came in as a guest to the congregation, dressed as King David. A leader in the church introduced me. She said, "It is with extreme pleasure and excitement, Trinity Church, that we welcome this day the grand patriarch of our faith, the unifying king of Israel, the musician extraordinaire, and the prophet poetic of the pre-exile age. We welcome to the Trinity pulpit the son of Jesse, a ruler of Israel. Let us stand up on our feet and welcome our guest, King David.")

I want to take this moment and opportunity to thank your pastor for allowing me to stand before you on this day. It's a blessing to be in the house of God. I greet you with the words from my people, who are your people, the word of *Shalom*, which means peace, that the peace of God will be upon you and upon your children, and upon your children's children.

It is the Holy Spirit that has allowed me to be released from the battlements of heaven to be with you on this day. Many of you know me as King David. I do not have that title anymore, for I just serve in heaven as a servant, giving glory to our God all day and all night.

The title *king* is not appropriate for me. It was a title that was given and bestowed upon me by the great Samuel, that I would be the unifier, the leader of Israel. Many of you have heard the redacted version of my story, but the story that I tell you today is closer to the truth and reality of who I am and the experience that I had as a person walking upon this earth. My story is a scandal, a scandal of epic proportions.

I was a child in the small, dusty village of Bethlehem. It was a place that rarely anyone visited. It never fell on any map. There was no reason to come to this place, which we like to call the house of bread. Bethlehem was a unique and interesting space to grow up in. I had older brothers. They were much larger than me. I served in the wilderness taking care of my father's sheep.

One day I was told that I must rush home, for my father wanted to see me. I did not want to leave my assignment with the sheep, but I made it home quickly, as the messenger told me that it was an emergency. When I came into the house I saw a gentlemen, tall, black, dressed in priestly garb, and I realized it was the great priest, sage, and purveyor of the word by the name of Samuel. My brothers were all on one side, all of them looking at me rather strangely; my father had a frown upon his face. I later found out that my father did not believe I had the capacity to lead anybody.

Samuel looked at me and he took a horn of oil, and he poured it on my head, and he began to cry. He said that I would be elevated to be the unifier of Israel. I still had the stench of the wilderness on my clothes, but now the sweetness and the smell of the anointed oil was mixed in with the stench of the wild. I did not realize that would be my story for the rest of my life—the smell of the anointing and the stench of the wild. My life would always be caught between the contradiction of my human proclivity and my divine assignment.

After the anointing, I was working with my brothers, for they had all enlisted in the army. There was this gigantic champion of a man who was taunting the armies of Israel. They called him Goliath. No one wanted to go before him; the size and the width of this man! Maybe it was just foolishness and immaturity, but I didn't like the fact that this giant was taunting our people. I don't know where I got the so-called courage. Perhaps it was the Spirit of God, but really I believe it was the foolishness of my youth. I was willing to step in front of this monster of a man.

Now you have not really been told the whole story. I understand that there are priests, and preachers, and prophets who talk about me and my five smooth stones, and how I took a slingshot and knocked down Goliath. If I may, I will tell you what really happened. I closed my eyes, and I threw a rock, and it just so happened to hit this giant of a man between the eyes. In the hoopla of the moment, people carried me and said that I had defeated Goliath. In reality, it was luck and the Spirit of God.

I was whisked into the palace at that time, and a gentleman by the name of Saul became my mentor and my nemesis all at the same time. I was a young man who loved to play the harp, and Saul had these episodes where you could see his face change from a moment of being lucid and then moving to his madness. Only my harp playing calmed his spirit. When they brought me back after the defeat of Goliath, something happened in the spirit of Saul.

I have to be quite honest with you. When they brought me back into Jerusalem, carrying me on the shoulders of soldiers, I was excited; but what really got me excited was when all those sisters were shouting my name. I have to be honest. I loved the ladies, and to hear them say, "David has killed tens of thousands, but Saul has only killed his thousands." Many of those women looked at me, and I looked at them, and we found our way to quiet places in Jerusalem. I cannot tell you the number, but it was beyond the number that I can count on my hands. Some of them thought that one day they would be queen, and I did not dissuade them of that idea.

There I was, working in the palace with my mentor and nemesis at the same time, when the madness of Saul came upon him one day. While my back was turned, he threw a spear at me—twice. I turned and looked at him. He stared at me and said, "Oops." At that moment I knew that my time was limited and that our relationship would not last very long, but I have always loved Saul, and I've always respected him. I have a great love for his family, especially Jonathan, who always supported me throughout all of my trials in Israel.

Once I became king, I brought in the Ark of the Covenant. It was me who led military excursion after military excursion. God gave me a strategic mind, but something happens to men when they are elevated. Their ego has a tendency to outstrip their God. I believed that I was king and that everything I surveyed was mine. I thought I could do no wrong because I didn't know what defeat tasted like. I had never had the moment where I had to bow down to anyone. Since I was small, I was lifted up as the one who was able to go against all enemies of Israel.

I ended up as king, making sure I hired the right people. There was one brother I hired that was an amazing gentleman, a fearless warrior. His name was Uriah. Uriah would step before the enemies of Israel, even if he was the only one, lift his sword, and go directly into battle. He was fearless. I'd never seen anyone with such boldness. He was not even an Israelite. He said, "I am loyal to you, David, because I believe in you."

We sent him out one day on an excursion to fight the enemies because we were taking over, expanding our territory. I think in your modern language you call it re-gentrification. We were taking land that people already had, and we were claiming it for ourselves. Uriah went out and did what he always did with his brilliant military mind. I stayed back at the palace because I was king. I stood on the balcony looking across the horizon of all Jerusalem, every building that I had built, the peace that I had brought, all that I had done as king.

As I stared across the landscape, my eyes stopped when I saw a woman on the roof bathing in a tub. Her beauty was absolutely magnificent. She was not clothed, and I knew from my upbringing that one is not supposed to gaze upon the nakedness of another, but I didn't care. I figured, I'm king. I can do what I want to do. My eyes would not break as I looked at this sister. Coffee black skin, the water dripping down off her shoulder, the curve upon her hips. I began to think to myself, "Who is she?" And "She needs to be with me." I leaned over to one of the guards, and the guard told me she was Uriah's wife, Bathsheba. I didn't care because I was king. I told them to go and get her for me. She was brought by guard into the palace, and we spent the night together. Even though she was experiencing her monthly cycle, I did not care. After I was done with her, she went home. There was no love. It was just one of the things I could do as king. Being king had benefits.

I received word not too long after that she was pregnant. I thought about falling before the altar and repenting before God, but then my ego and political mind popped up.

I needed to cover up the sin that I had committed. I hatched a plan to kill the most loyal soldier I had ever known. I killed Uriah. Not with my own hands, but as he made a charge toward the enemy, I gave orders for his soldiers to pull back, and he was killed with the sword of the enemy. They brought his body back, and we had a state-sponsored funeral, and I did the eulogy. I stood over his body, and I talked about what a great man you are, Uriah, how awesome you are, how loyal you are, how there was no other man like you in all of Israel who has ever fought—all as his wife wore black mourning clothes, sitting in the front row. Knowing she was pregnant, and knowing I had killed him. I married her several days later. Not because I loved her. There was no love in the relationship. It was all about politics, making sure things looked right. If you do not remember anything that I say to you on this day, I say to you, what you do in the dark, at some point, will come to light. That your neighbor may not know, but Yahweh sees all.

I was comfortable for a while until the great prophet, Nathan, showed up and began to tell me a parable of a man who had offended and disgraced a poor man by stealing one of his sheep. Even though he had the resources to provide sheep to anyone that he wanted, he had to steal from someone else. As he told the details of the story, I became enraged, and I said, "Find me that man and he shall die right now."

Nathan turned his head to the side, slightly smiled, slowly moved and took his hand out and looked at his nails, then looked up at me and said, "Thou art the man." It was like someone had put a stake through my heart. Then he went on to say, "Your family shall be destroyed because of your actions." How can a man be a man when he destroys his family? When his ego is more important than the real calling God has given him?

Bathsheba gave birth to our child, and soon after that child came out of her womb the child took a breath, cried, and then was silent, and died in the birthing bed. I had to pick that tiny little baby up, and I cried because the baby in my hand was dead because of me. I buried the child. I went before God. I even wrote a psalm some of you recite to this day, "Create in me a clean heart and renew within me a right spirit." Things had already been put in motion. You can't wait 'til your children grow up to decide to be a dad.

The story that I do not want to share is my disgrace. You all love to talk about David, but you don't know my real story. When my daughter was born, we named her after the palm trees that sprout up next to the Nile. That's what *Tamar* means, that she was a child of promise. She was my little girl. My son Amnon . . . my son Amnon raped my daughter. My son violated my daughter, and it was a pain that I cannot describe. It was anger that I cannot even conceive of to this day. I pulled my sword; I ripped apart everything in the king's quarters. Then my ego outstripped my theology, and I didn't do anything.

Every girl deserves a father who will at least speak up. I was silent because I didn't want people to know there was something wrong in the palace. My daughter had more courage than her daddy. She put on sackcloth and ashes. What she was saying to everybody was, "Something's wrong in the palace." She was also telling me, "Father, you are dead to me. You did not speak up for me." She was saying to me, "I can handle it when you go out to battle. I can even excuse all of your indiscretions with women, but for you not to speak up when I was violated, I can never forgive you."

Her other brother, Absalom, told her she could live with him. She never entered the palace again. She never spoke to me for the rest of my life. Absalom, so angry with me, killed his brother. One son, Amnon, raped his sister. My other son, Absalom, killed his brother. I was in my chambers trying to figure out how this could happen to me. How could my children live and operate with such violation? Then I realized, they learned everything from me. They had watched their father take women out of other men's arms just so he could sleep with them. They watched their father kill men and then talk about the death. When Goliath fell, you don't know the whole story. They lifted me up on their soldiers, yes, but I ran over to the body of Goliath as he was still unconscious, and I cut his head off. I brought the head to Saul. I danced with his head, the blood lust on my heart. Something that you can never get back dies in you when you take someone's life.

I know in this modern age—as I had a conversation with your pastor—that many of you like to watch a show called *Scandal*. It's really just a reworking of my story. There was another show your pastor talked about called *Game of Thrones*. One family called the Starks. Another family called the Lannisters. It's all about how people in one family are trying to get to the throne. As he told me the story, I said, "This story is plagiarism. They are just retelling my story. One son who is involved in incest and rape, another son who kills that son, a daughter who has been exiled, wives, and many wives.

Absalom, after killing his brother, made it his life's mission to kill and destroy his father. He found his way into the Israelite community, telling people that, "If you really want someone to serve as king, you need someone who will listen to you. If I were judge, if I were leader, you wouldn't have to wait for a year or two just to meet with the king." He stole the hearts of people. When I heard that he was on his way to take me out, I ran from the palace and hid in the forest.

Then the most loyal of all advisers, Ahithophel, gave him advice. He was the one who we all trusted. He was loyal, not to me. I don't even know if he was loyal to Absalom. He was loyal to himself. He told Absalom, "If you really want people to know that you are alienated from your father, then take the secondary wives and have sex with them in public." They built a tent on top of the palace, and there was Absalom with my secondary wives. That term, *secondary wife*, is a polite political term. I believe you all have different terms for people who are seen in this vein. Everyone watched the debauchery of my son, which he had learned from me.

I was hiding in the woods, and Absalom was lurking and looking with his men for me. Riding into the forest one day on his mule, when he saw my men, his hair got caught in a thicket. He had been growing those locks since he was eight. Now he was hanging from a tree, I was told. My men were not going to kill him; but one of my lieutenants, Joab, who was my cousin (a shrewd political character), wanted to put down the coup d'état, so he killed his cousin, thrusting three spears into his heart. I remember as if it were yesterday, the Cushite coming over the hill, running as fast as he could, saying, "Your enemies have been vanquished, oh king. They are now gone."

I said, "What of my son?"

"Your son has been vanquished, the enemy of the king."

When your family is your enemy, this is a position that you do not want anyone ever to be in. I fell back; I remember the breath falling out of my body. I remember calling out, "Absalom! Absalom! My son, it should have been me, not you. I caused this." I wanted to know where his body was. They told me they threw his body in an unmarked grave. I couldn't even bury my son in the way that he deserved to be buried. All because I thought I was king, and I didn't know who was king. I served the King, but I thought I was king. I was never king. I had king proclivities, but I was more of a glorified pimp than I was a king.

I know that in your tradition you speak of "good news" when you come to worship. How can there be good news in such a story, a story of a man that stands before you broken? Where is the good news? Your pastor told me a tale of a preacher by the name of Fred Craddock—you all have interesting names in this country. I guess he's a sage, or an elder, preacher, priest, who was traveling from L.A. to a place called New York on this vehicle that flies in the air—which is unbelievable to me. I don't like boats, and you all get in tubes that fly in the air.

There he was. He said he was in this vehicle. He was sharing with the person next to him that he was going to visit a sick friend, who he was thankful was now well, and what a blessing it is to have the opportunity to be in the presence of someone you love. He just politely asked this woman next to him, "Where are you going?"

She sadly said, "I am going to see my father." Knowing that he was a minister, she said, "The last time I saw my father, I walked out the door, slammed it in his face before I walked out, and said, 'Go to Hell. I never want to see you again.'"

Mr. Craddock, attempting to be priestly, said to this woman, "Aren't you glad that you have the opportunity to see your father again?"

She said, "My father died two weeks ago. The last time, and last moment, and the last thing he ever heard in his spirit was that his daughter told him to go to hell."

Is it worth it? Is it really worth it to hold on to the hate that long? To keep the grudge like a yoke around your neck; is it really worth it? No one knows what tomorrow brings.

I said that there is good news in my story. They gave me a state funeral and sang songs about the greatness of David, but that is not the good news. They call my name every time they speak of Israel, but that is not the good news. The symbol of Israel is called the Star of David, but that is not the good news. The good news is when I died, and that great light opened up in my spirit, and I made my way to that place called heaven, I could not walk through the gates because I saw my little girl. She wasn't wearing sackcloth and ashes. She was saying, "Welcome home, Daddy." I saw Absalom, who hated me—not with a sword or a spear, but with his arms open saying, "Welcome home, Daddy." I saw Amnon, no longer with demons, saying, "Welcome home, Daddy." I saw Bathsheba saying, "Welcome home." I saw my little baby smiling and cooing, saying "Welcome home." Everyone I had mistreated said, "Welcome home."

I wept and fell on my knees and said I would rather spend my eternity in hell because I cannot face those I have mistreated. That's when a man walked out who had feet of burnished bronze and hair of lamb's wool. He said, "You don't know me, but you met my father. I want you to know that now you know what grace is, that I kept you even though you couldn't keep yourself, that I loved you even though you didn't love yourself. That I walked with you even when you didn't know I was walking with you. That you, now, understand what grace is. That I love you beyond the understanding of what you know love to be."

No longer am I called King David, I'm just David. Now when you make it to heaven, I will greet you. I'll be next to my girl, and I'll be next to my children. I'll be next to everybody that I mistreated. There's a section for where we are. It's a section for those who like to praise God for God's grace. All we do all day long is we say, "Holy! Holy! Holy! Holy!" We praise God in the morning, and we praise God in the evening, because every time I get flashbacks of what I was, and what I did, and how God continues to love me, all I can say is, "Holy! Holy!"

I know it is not the tradition of this church. I came here because the Holy Spirit released me to talk to you. I've done more dirt than anybody, but this altar is for you. For those of you who've got dirt under your fingernails. For those of you who've got the smell of the anointing and the stench of the wilderness, this altar is for you. For those who've held onto grudges and pains that you cannot release, this altar is for you.

The pastor said that I could do this. If you want to be released because you know that your biology has sometimes outstripped your theology. That you've done dirt, and there have been people who have been victims of what you have done. This altar is open right now. If one of our ministers, these ministers of this church, would be so kind as to pray for you, I thank you that I had the time to speak with you. Shalom.

Sermon 3

MINISTRY AND OUR MANDATE

Proverbs 31

(This sermon was preached in the weeks following the murder of Michael Brown and the protests in Ferguson, Missouri, in the fall of 2014.)

> Speak up for those who cannot speak for themselves,
> for the rights of all who are destitute.
> Speak up and judge fairly;
> defend the rights of the poor and the needy.
> (Proverbs 31:8–9 NIV)

> Speak up for the people who have no voice,
> for the rights of all, the down-and-outers.
> Speak out for justice!
> Stand up for the poor and the destitute!
> (vv. 8–9 The Message)

I'd like for us to focus on the subject of moments, movements, ministry, and our mandate. Moments, movements, ministry, and our mandate.

Here's a man named Langston Hughes. He's considered one of the greatest poets this country has ever created, the Harlem renaissance writer and brilliant cultural critic. I believe it was sometime during the 1930s that he penned a poem entitled "Harlem." I believe it's apropos for our understanding of our current crisis in this America, the yet-to-be-United States of America. Langston Hughes posed a question that still rings down through the annals of history. He asked,

> What happens to a dream deferred?
>
> Does it dry up
> like a raisin in the sun?
> Or fester like a sore—
> and then run?
> Does it stink like rotten meat?
> Or crust and sugar over—
> like a syrupy sweet?
>
> Maybe it just sags
> like a heavy load.
>
> Or [like in Ferguson] does it explode?

The writer James Baldwin probably gives the framing that is most apropos to our understanding of our current crisis. Baldwin said, "To be a Negro in this country and relatively conscious is to be in a rage almost all the time" (*Time*, August 20, 1965).

We find ourselves once again peering into the abyss, and the abyss seems to be staring back at us with nothing but darkness. Death, destruction, fires, frustration, pain; pain caused by political exclusion, rage birthed from scars of years of neglect and resentment. Weeping can be heard across the land because of the injury not to the body but to our soul. If a psychologist were to look at us collectively, not only as a country but as a community, they would say that we have post-traumatic-stress disorder, PTSD; but I would say we have PTRD, Post Traumatic Race Disorder.

On a daily basis, we witness our own lynching; but we witness micro-lynchings every day. If you are a person of color and you are relatively conscious, you will find yourself witnessing the micro-lynching of your own soul just living in America. People will say peculiar and strange things to you. They will say, "Oh, Otis, you speak so articulately. You speak so well," as if being Black and articulate is an oxymoron. Then, that same type of pain can turn inward into our community, where many women have been defined, not simply by their intellect and their spirituality, but defined by their physicality—where your own people can look at you and even say, "You are pretty for a Black girl."

Being a person who is relatively conscious, you will witness micro-lynching day to day. In other words, America sometimes will force you to taste its own strange fruit, and we watch and bear witness to pundits who dissect our psyches and academics who analyze our culture, politicians who dismiss our claim upon democracy. It's a strange affair to be Black and live in America, and even stranger to be Black and a person of faith in these yet-to-be-United States, to carry around the burden of a socially constructed idea called *race* and yet be filled with a divinely inspired mandate to eradicate all limitations to the human soul. Being Black means you are born with a Blues song tattooed on your heart, and at the same time you still have a Gospel shout that is welling up in your soul about to come out.

Another way to say it is that we live with repression and revelation simultaneously swimming in the same tributary of our spirit. There is nothing more confusing to the postmodern personality, to the millennial sojourner, than to have to exist between the strange life of dealing with your Blues and Gospel all the time. Madness and ministry, chaos and Christ.

My father heard an elder in Georgia say it this way. When he asked her, "How are you doing, Mother?" She said, "I'm living between Oh Lord and Thank you, Jesus."

For the most part, many of us are living in between, not quite at "Oh Lord" and not quite at "Thank you, Jesus," but somewhere in between. If you choose to be conscious and understand the system at work, study the history of repression, know what hate will do when it's turned inward onto your own spirit, examine the forces of consumption, get a picture of colonialism, understand the root of imperialism, and begin to deconstruct the powers that be. At some point, you will find yourself leaning upon the Blues and facing despair, and wondering if you should give up.

I heard many young men and women—sisters and brothers from Ferguson—who were raising a question, who had never come into a place of worship. They would not walk into a temple or a synagogue or a mosque, or find themselves in a community of accountability such as Trinity United Church of Christ, and they were shouting at the tops of their lungs. Their voices were now hoarse. Their fingers were now sore because they had been posting so long, frustrated by what they were seeing. The question that they were raising is where is God in all of this? Where is the church? Where have the leaders gone? Our institutions have failed us. I am brought to this particular text in the midst of this because I believe it speaks to our crisis at hand.

Go home when you have time and begin reading at the top of chapter 31. This is not about a father speaking to a son. This is about a mother talking to her son. This is a mother, a queen mother, sharing with a king, King Lemuel, who is about to rise and become the one who sits upon the throne. She is trying to tell him that, when you move into that position, there are certain things that you must know boy. And if I may give my translation, I believe that Momma was talking this way to her child, saying,

> Boy, speak out for those who cannot speak. Make sure that you speak up for the rights of all who are poor and who are destitute. Speak out and open your mouth for justice and for those who cannot open their mouths, because not too long ago we were not in the royal court. There were other people before you were born who opened up their mouth so that you now have the opportunity to sit on this throne. I say to you as your mother, to my son, that I want you to know that life for me ain't been no crystal stair. I want you to understand that I know you will hold the title King, but all of your people were not given the opportunity to hold that title. There was a time that you were birthed out of pain and trouble and sorrow and blues, so I don't want you to ever forget. When you get to your position and sit on the throne, don't you think that you did it all by yourself. You are sitting on a throne that has been fertilized with the blood of people that you don't even know. I speak this wisdom into your spirit, and this is the mandate of Israel. This is the ethic that is the core of the faith, the responsibility of every person in the community, the tikkun as the Hebraic people call it, the repairing of the breach.

When you see yourself apart, as connected in this deep way to a lineage, it changes the way that you look at the world. If you do not see yourself connected to anything, you will try to find a way to bring your voice to the forefront. It was Dr. King who said that a riot is the language of the unheard, that the only reason that people burn things is because they have been excluded, and they do not have the capacity yet to communicate what they are truly feeling in their spirit. When a child cannot communicate, the child will throw a fit and throw and break some things just to get your attention. I do not want anyone to focus on Ferguson and just focus on fires. Yes, there are fires that happened in Ferguson, but that is not the whole story. For the last several months, there have been people who have been protesting, and teaching, and organizing, and there was no violence that broke out, but when the news came by, the news trucks kept driving because they were looking for something else.

The good news is that there were young activists—Black and white and Latino and Asian, Internet activists, Eco-activists, occupy people, socialists sitting down with Christians and LGBTQ people, sitting down with socially conscious evangelicals—all together because they recognize that bullets do not ask your zip code or your orientation. Police misconduct and accountability can be transformed only when we recognize that it is *our* problem. If you relegate it to just one community, it's eventually in some form or fashion going to visit your community. We need to see that we are all interconnected and that we are connected together; this can only happen when this ethic to stand up for the vulnerable, this sacred mandate, operates within our soul.

Proverbs 31 is just simply saying speak up for those who are poor, those who do not have a voice for themselves. It is a mother telling a privileged son that your privilege was not always there before you. There was a time when you did not have this before you were born. There are mandates that we must understand, that Ferguson is a moment, but we must understand that we can connect it to a larger movement. Anytime you start saying that nothing happened until Ferguson, obviously you lack an understanding of history. You really don't know what has been happening since we have arrived on these shores known as North America, and that God has given us a mandate to make our history sacred.

What is implicit in the text is that the mother understands that the child has been raised in a household, and in a village that has a story, and that history is sacred. In this day and age, we have people who believe we are an anomaly, and that we have no historical context. We raise this question as others did. They said, "Where is God? Where is the faith community? Are they present? What is going on? There is nobody fighting. There is nobody leading."

Well, let me say this emphatically. First of all, stop waiting for somebody to lead. You have the intelligence. You have the capacity to lead yourself. If you're always looking for somebody to lead you, then you've got to be careful because they may lead you astray. You've got to be able to have your own empowerment and not depend on someone else to empower you. Do not say that we have not been fighting. Do not say the Black church didn't do anything.

Let me break down the history very quickly. You must understand that your history is sacred. It is not the silence of the Black church. No. It is the fact that we do not have a microphone that is as loud as some of those in the media and those who are on The Word Network and sit in big gold chairs.

We may not have the noise of others, but you must understand that, since we landed on these shores in 1619, and our toes touched the red clay of Georgia and South Carolina, we have been fighting. Three hundred slave insurrections have been recorded in history, and only three of them did not occur in church. Any time people of color got together and we started worshiping our God, we knew that our God did not intend for us to be in bondage. We were fighting from the moment that we arrived here.

You may not know that as a result of one of those insurrections, Louisiana almost became free territory for Black people, and that Haiti almost became an ally of Louisiana.

You may not know that South Carolina almost became an African Free State.

You may not know that Sojourner Truth was raped several times, but after her rape she did not fall into despair. She was still able to stand before men and women and say, "Ain't I a woman?"

You may not know Robert Smalls was able to liberate a confederate ship, sail it from South Carolina all the way to Washington, D.C., present it as a gift to Abraham Lincoln, and say, "Look what our people can do."

You may not know of a woman by the name of Lucy Craft Laney, who started the first private kindergarten in Georgia. She had a little mentee by the name of Mary McLeod Bethune, to whom she said, "When you get older, you build a school to expand the minds of people of African descent."

You may not know a child in Saint Anne Bay, Jamaica, who read a book called *Up From Slavery*. After reading it, he got on a boat and made his way to America and formed the Universal Negro Improvement Association. His name was Marcus Garvey.

You may not know a Howard University graduate, a man by the name of Mordecai Wyatt Johnson, who went to the Harlem Renaissance writers in 1926 and placed them at Howard so that they could run different departments— so Charles Hamilton Houston and Alain Locke and

E. Franklin Frazier could educate an entire generation—and Thurgood Marshall could come through Howard Law School and be educated by Charles Hamilton Houston.

What I am trying to say is this: do not act like you did it by yourself, like you are the first person to ever do it. You come from a lineage of people who have been fighting day in and day out to change this country so that it will live up to its creed.

Don't you ever say we have not been fighting. We have been fighting since the day we arrived on these shores. Fighting is in your DNA. Fighting is who we are. America would not be America today if it did not have an encounter with people of African descent. You can't build a nation unless you have ingenuity, creativity, and labor. Don't tell me we "have not" because the record of history is true. The record of history cannot be denied. For those of you who have fallen into a level of cynicism, thinking that we "cannot" and "nothing will work," let me tell you, when you get up tomorrow on Monday morning, it will be December first. That means nothing to you, but let me break it down, because you should shout every December first. December first was the day a little woman by the name of Rosa Parks sat down so you could stand up.

When you get up tomorrow, you say, "God, I thank you for Rosa. That she could sit down so I could stand up." And only God can teach you to do two things that sound contradictory at the same time, that she sat down and stood up at the same time. We must make our history sacred.

Growing up in Cleveland, I used to have to go to many bar mitzvahs and bat mitzvahs. I used to love going there because they always had good food. But it amazed me that every child—woman and man—when they moved from that rite of passage from age twelve to age thirteen, they had to talk about their history. They said you can't be a man or a woman unless you know your ancestors. You cannot be a man or a woman, they would say, until you know who stands behind you.

That is why, biblically, they always say who begot so and so. You pass it over in the Bible, but it is important to know that you are not the only one. You come out of a lineage that births you into this world. Here we are at this moment in Ferguson, and we are frustrated as a people and as a nation, saying why did it happen? Why do Black lives matter? America, because of its racialized imagination, has always tried to focus on the fact that there is something wrong, especially with Black males and Black men. It's not anything new. It's not anything new at all.

You must understand that this all changed in 1863, in the breakout of the Civil War. Previous to 1863, if you wanted somebody to do some work in your house and raise your child, somebody that you deeply trusted, you found somebody of African descent. Something happened after 1863, because with emancipation in 1865, all of a sudden you witness and see that all of the literature changes from describing Black people as loyal and having ingenuity and creativity. You need to read the literature to see, all of a sudden, they are criminals. The only reason the literature changed is because Black people were competing for labor with white people. There had to be a system created to say that you should not hire the person who built the country in the first place, since they have more experience than you.

An entire system was built to say that you're a criminal. If you tell a lie long enough, even those who are being lied about will believe the lie. That is why, even to this day, there are some people even in this church growing up in Trinity, there are some of our young people, who believe that doing well in school is acting white. Are you out of your mind? You built pyramids. Are you out of your mind? Do you know who you are? It's not acting white. You're acting as a child of God. You're acting out of your lineage and your history, but we have heard a lie so long that we believe the lie.

In order for us to correct this, I believe we must make our history sacred. It is a mandate from God. Some might say, "Reverend, doesn't that divide us? Shouldn't we all be one?" You know what, no one ever has a problem when the Irish have their March on Saint Patrick's day. We will turn a river green, and we will celebrate everything. I have no problem with somebody celebrating their heritage. We have no problem when you drive down to what is called Chinatown—celebrating. You have no problem when you go down to Little Village—celebrating. Have no problem when you go down to Ukraine Village. No problem, but all of a sudden, when you start talking about us, it's going to be a division. I'm here to let you know that when we make our history sacred, no longer will we allow the lies of someone else to define who we are.

When we make our history sacred, you will not call a woman a *B*. You will not call your brother an *N*. When we make our history sacred, there will be some things we will not accept. You have a mandate to know your history. Reject the racialized imagination of America. When police officers see a young man of color, every brother in here knows, that you have to carry yourself differently, because you don't want to get taken out or shot. If you're a certain size, you really have to carry yourself differently, because you know that people look at you a particular way. All of a sudden, you have to shift your physicality to ensure that you are communicating in a way, non-verbally, that you will not be a threat to somebody who thinks that you are a threat because of their demented psychology. And because of their demented psychology, they now have a messed-up sociology, because now they see everybody who looks like you—even though they don't know you—they see you a particular way. And because of that messed-up psychology, they have a messed-up anthropology. Their anthropology is now framed so that they don't understand the humanity that comes out of you.

The real reason is this: when you have no theology, then you have a messed-up psychology, and you cannot have the right sociology, and you will have a skewed anthropology. The mandate that we have is a mandate to make our history sacred, but not only a mandate to have our history sacred. We also have a mandate to speak up for those who have no voice. The mother is trying to tell the son that he must alleviate suffering—a mandate to alleviate suffering. It's good to know your history, but if you know your history and there is no action, then you really don't know your history.

You must also alleviate the suffering, and not just the suffering in your community. The mandate is that wherever there is suffering you must relieve that suffering. That the faith community should be designed around the alleviation of suffering and compassion for those who are destitute. This is what this mother was attempting to say to the son. Reverend Tony Campolo, that great sociologist and preacher out of Philadelphia, who I have quoted many times, tells the story of when he was in Hawaii. I believe he was in Hawaii for some type of conference or revival. He was at a diner around 3:00 a.m. in Hawaii, minding his own business, eating his food, and as he was in there, two women from the red light district came in to sit down to eat.

He overheard the two women, who were defined as prostitutes, talking, and one of the women was saying, "Tomorrow is my birthday."

The other woman jokingly said, "Nobody cares if it's your birthday."

She said, "I don't care. It's my birthday, and I'm going to celebrate my birthday and I'm going to say happy birthday to myself."

They eventually left to go on about their business, and Reverend Campolo then asked the owner of the diner, "Do they come in here all the time?"

He said, "Yes, they come in here every single night at about the same time and order about the same thing."

Campolo said, "Well, I want to do something. My name is Reverend Campolo. I'm a preacher and I believe the Holy Spirit just spoke to me. I want to throw a party for that sister who said it was her birthday."

The owner looked at him and said, "You want to throw a party for a prostitute?"

He said, "I want to throw a party for a prostitute."

The owner was wondering and said, "You serve a God who throws a party for a prostitute?"

He said, "Yes, I'm telling you. I'll get the cake. I'll pay for everything. We're going to throw a party for this sister, because I believe that we should celebrate and alleviate some of the suffering in her life. I don't know her but we should throw a party."

Eventually, the owner agreed that they would do this. They called up all of her friends and her associates and what not, and the people who meet in that diner at around that time, and told them they were going to have a surprise party for this particular sister who worked the street. When 3:00 came the next day, 3:00 a.m., they were all in the diner hiding in and around behind the counter. She came in and saw streamers and balloons. They flicked on more lights, and said, "Happy Birthday! Surprise!" The woman was completely bewildered. They rolled out a huge cake, three tiers, that said "Happy Birthday" with her name on it. They told her to blow out the candles. She blew out the candles, and she started to weep. She wrapped her arms around the cake and started to hug the cake.

She cried and cried, and she said, "No one has ever thrown a party for me. No one has ever told me happy birthday." She looked with tears in her eyes at the owner and Reverend Campolo and said, "Can I take the cake home?"

They said yes. She carried the cake, still hugging it, and walked out of the diner. Everyone was stunned. They didn't know what to do and didn't know what to say.

The owner said, "Hey, preacher. You've got us all here together. Shouldn't we pray or something?"

He said, "Yeah, I guess so."

The owner said, "Well, you the preacher, so you need to do the praying." They got all into a circle but they decided to do a round-robin prayer where each person would say what they are thankful for. Here they are, a circle; some prostitutes, some drug dealers, some drug addicts, and a preacher and a diner owner, all in a circle together.

Campolo wasn't sure who said it but somebody said, "I'm thankful for a God who throws parties for prostitutes." That's the kind of God we serve. A God who is willing, a God who sees the pain of those whom no one else sees. The question is, shall we be the kind of church that is willing to throw parties for prostitutes, and willing to throw parties for drug addicts, and willing to throw parties for prisoners, willing to throw parties for the homeless? Are we willing to reach out to those and alleviate suffering? I believe our God calls us, not just to throw a party for yourself but to throw a party for those in need.

I know that there is somebody that's saying it right now, saying, "I appreciate what you're saying, but can't we hear a happy sermon? Can't you just tell me I'm blessed and highly favored? Can't you just tell me I'm going to get a new house, going to get a brand new car, going to hit the lotto? Just tell me everything's going to be all right, and all I have to do is call God's name and everything will be fine. Can't you just do that?" No, I can't do that, because the God that I serve didn't promise you a house, didn't promise you a car, didn't promise you a new job. The God I serve did promise you peace, did promise you joy, did promise you grace, and God did promise you mercy. God didn't promise money in your pocket, but God did promise you to be able to walk through the valley of the shadow of death and fear no evil.

The God that we serve is calling us to have a mandate to alleviate suffering—a mandate to make our history sacred, a mandate to alleviate suffering—but the final thing is simply this: a mandate to dream a new world. Speak up for those who can't speak. Dream of a world that has yet to be created. Don't wait for somebody to do it. Do it yourself. God has given you the tools. The world is difficult. Cynicism is not an option. Cynicism has no place in our heart. Despair has not been granted access to our souls. Cynicism and despair are enemies of love and justice.

Some are saying, "I don't see any miracles, Reverend." Well, I see a miracle every day. Every day I wake up I see a miracle. I see a miracle in here. Every time I see our young people, I'm looking at a miracle, because I do not know what the future holds for them, but I know who holds their future. There is a poet who says children are not your children. They come through you but not from you. They are life's longing for life, that we are the bows and they are the arrows, that they have been bequeathed a great heritage.

As a matter of fact, I'm going to ask all of those college students to stand up for a moment. Stand up. Power has been granted to you. You have a mandate, a charge to keep, a covenant to carry, a calling to fulfill, a promise to live. Your opportunities, the fact that you are in school, it is a privilege. Not all of us can make it to college. Not all of us will go, but you are there. You must know who is there when you walk into the classroom. Know that there is a cloud of witnesses with you who are standing in the balcony, smiling and cheering you on. Every test you take, Frederick Douglass is saying, "Go ahead with your bad self." Every book you read, Harriet Tubman is saying, "Go ahead with your bad self." There's a cloud of witnesses with you every time you step in.

Don't say, "I'm by myself." You are never by yourself. We have fought. We have prayed so that you can have that desk, have that moment, have that class, have that time. We rest our hopes on you. Do not become discouraged. Do not be dismayed, whatever is taught, God will make a way. Do not be discouraged. Do not be disheartened. God will make a way. I want you to know, may the Lord bless you real good. May the road rise to meet you. May the wind be at your back. But I stop by here to let you know that love reigns, that compassion is king, that justice rules, and faith abounds. Peace is promised. God has bequeathed something great to you. Thank you. You may be seated. God has called you.

We will all leave this place, but we are turning something over to you, and if you are brave enough to take what you have and to turn it over to God, God will create something new. What is this newness that God will create? God will take your gifts and draw something that you have never seen, paint something that no one could paint, write something that no one else could write; but you must release what God has given you and turn it over to God

I want you to know that you've got to take your gifts, turn them over to God. Go out into the storm and let God beat across the canvas of your soul, and do something that you never thought that God could do. It may seem like a storm, but I'm so glad that in Ferguson there are young activists and God is painting something new. I'm so glad that in New York there are young activists and God is doing something new. I'm so glad in Oakland there are young people and God is doing something new. I'm so glad in Chicago that there are activists and God is doing something new. God is painting a new picture in our lives if we're willing to trust in God. Let God paint. Go out into the storm. There's a mandate for our history to be sacred. There's a mandate for us to alleviate suffering. There is a mandate to dream a new world. Turn over your canvas to God.

Sermon 4

HOW TO GET AWAY WITH MURDER
Matthew 2:13–18 and Luke 2:8–14

(Sermon preached immediately following the grand jury findings on the Michael Brown case in November 2014.)

Now after they had left, an angel of the Lord appeared to Joseph in a dream and said, "Get up, take the child and his mother, and flee to Egypt [another translation says flee to Africa] and remain there until I tell you; for Herod is about to search for the child, to destroy him." Then Joseph got up, took the child and his mother by night, and went to Egypt [went to Africa] and remained there until the death of Herod. This was to fulfill what had been spoken by the Lord through the prophet, "Out of Egypt [out of Africa] I have called my son."

When Herod saw that he had been tricked by the wise men, he was infuriated, and he sent and killed all the children in and around Bethlehem who were two years old or under, according to the time that he had learned from the wise men. Then was fulfilled what had been spoken through the prophet Jeremiah:

"A voice was heard in Ramah,
    wailing and loud lamentation,
Rachel weeping for her children;
    she refused to be consoled, because they were no
more."

(Matthew 2:13–18)

In that region there were shepherds living in the fields, keeping watch over their flock by night. Then an angel of the Lord stood before them, and the glory of the Lord shone around them, and they were terrified. But the angel said to them, "Do not be afraid; for see—I am bringing you good news of great joy for all the people: to you is born this day in the city of David a Savior, who is the Messiah, the Lord. This will be a sign for you: you will find a child wrapped in bands of cloth and lying in a manger." And suddenly there was with the angel a multitude of the heavenly host, praising God and saying,
> "Glory to God in the highest heaven,
>   and on earth peace among those whom he favors!"

(Luke 2:8–14)

Let me read part of the Matthew text using the OM3 (Otis Moss III) translation:

When Herod saw that he had been tricked by the wise men who came from the East, he was infuriated and put forth a policy to leave no child behind, and he sent the Roman security forces, and they killed children in the poor city of Bethlehem. No one was indicted for the crime. This fulfilled what had been spoken through the prophet Jeremiah: "A voice is heard at Ramah, wailing and loud lamentation, Rachel weeping for her children; she refused to be consoled because they are no more."

I'd like for us to focus on the subject of how to get away with murder. If you could turn to your neighbor at this time, just turn and look at your neighbor, smile at your neighbor, and say, "Neighbor . . . O neighbor . . . Rachel . . . is weeping . . . and she cannot . . . be consoled."

Find another neighbor and say, "Neighbor . . . O neighbor . . . Herod . . . is in a position . . . of power . . . but God . . . has all authority."

How to get away with murder. There is a woman by the name of Shonda Rhimes who created several popular television shows: *Grey's Anatomy*, *Scandal*, and another called *How to Get Away with Murder*. For some this has become appointment television. They cannot miss an episode and will even skip coming to choir rehearsal if there is a new episode on. It is not my desire or duty to lift up any type of cultural nuances about these television shows, to do an examination culturally or theologically of what Shonda Rhimes has done.

I believe, as I looked at the scripture and rummaged through the basement of my own imagination, I found something, a parchment still heavy with dust, that I want to read for you today. It was an ancient news clipping from Palestine. It was from the most progressive Hebraic paper of the day. These news clippings come from the *Palestinian Defender*. From my understanding, it has been in operation since the time Pharaoh ordered the death of Hebrew children in Egypt. The paper has accurately chronicled the day-to-day struggle of Hebrew men and women for hundreds of years. If I may, I would like to read to you what I found. I believe it will be helpful for our understanding of the things that we struggle with on this day.

The clipping that I first found from the *Defender* reads as follows:

Eyewitness reports by numerous Hebrews state Roman security forces dressed in full-scale battle regalia, not peacekeeping attire, entered hundreds of Palestinian homes without a warrant, detaining families and separating children from their parents. Eyewitnesses report that children were killed under the orders of Herod, the alleged king of the Jews. A group of activists from the organization HLM, Hebrew Lives Matter, have filed a formal lawsuit in Rome demanding the Roman attorney general investigate these atrocities.

At the time of the printing of this report, the attorney general of Rome claimed he had no jurisdiction over religious groups, and all lawsuits must be filed in the jurisdiction of the governor by the name of Herod. The local prosecutor appointed by Herod has formed a grand jury to see if there is sufficient evidence to proceed with the trial. On this grand jury, there are nine Romans and three Palestinians who have been chosen to serve and accepted the service. The defender petitioned to sit in the rotunda of Herod's capital for the press conference after the grand jury determined the verdict. The paper will follow up with all the developments and make sure that the readers know what is happening in the community.

The next clipping that I found read this way:

The grand jury deliberated for only eight hours. The prosecutor, Leukenius, gave a long forty-minute statement. This is unusual, since prosecutors normally just simply state what the grand jury decided— which is 99 percent of the time to indict and allow the case to move forward. This prosecutor decided to place blame on the grand jury and the lack of evidence. According to the prosecutor, the eighteen witnesses to the atrocity were: 1) unreliable, 2) many already had previous run-ins with Palestinian security forces and had records and therefore could not be relied upon. We will keep you informed of further developments.

The next clipping that I found in the basement of my imagination reads this way:

> The *Defender* has obtained a portion of an article published in Rome by the conservative paper known as *Fox and Eagle News* that this reporter believes led to the refusal of the grand jury to indict. We have obtained a portion of it and have printed it for all of our readers in Palestine. It reads as follows:
>
> "The grand jury came to the correct and sane conclusion after reviewing all of the evidence. We, the editorial staff of *Fox and Eagle*, believe that instead of protest and weeping, the Hebrew community should be more concerned about Hebrew on Hebrew crime. There are more deaths at the hands of Hebrews than Roman soldiers.
>
> "Hebrews fill most of the Roman jails, and the high Hebrew unemployment rate has created a culture of poverty in the Hebrew community. Many Hebrews look for government handouts and seek to take instead of to earn. If Hebrews stopped listening to those radical racial leaders, such as Amos, Isaiah, Jeremiah, and the zealots, they would learn so much more to be successful. It should be noted that several of them are under investigation for tax evasion. More good Hebrews are needed, like

Zacchaeus the tax collector." The *Fox and Eagle*
report ends there.

The *Palestinian Defender* says this,

The *Defender*'s editorial staff believes not only have
the policies of Herod created the atmosphere of
death, but the mentality of prejudice in Rome cre-
ates a system where Hebrew children and boys are
targets for Roman security forces who are trained to
view Hebrew children as suspects. It is our belief a
movement must occur to tear down this system.

The next clipping that I found read this way:

There are several sources inside the palace of Herod
who claim Herod ordered Roman forces into Palestine because of fear of an uprising. Herod received
news from wise men from the East that a messiah
would be born. This would fit the description of Isaiah who stated that the government would be upon
his shoulders. The *Defender* plans to keep the reader
abreast of any new news of a messiah. If a messiah has
been born, this will mean a movement will take place
that will topple the Roman government and redeem
all humanity. We at the *Defender* will report any findings on this matter.

There end the clippings that I found, rummaging through
the basement of my imagination. What we realize by looking at the scripture is that Herod has figured out a way to
get away with murder. As you see, it is easy to get away
with murder when you are in a particular position and the

system works for you. It is easy to get away with murder when it is sanctioned by a system.

Look at the scripture and understand the context of what is happening here. Herod's position and policies support the Roman system. Jewish labor is necessary for Rome to develop, so it is important that Jews go to jail—to build Roman roads, to provide that labor to build the Roman Empire. There is an interest in saying that Hebrews have some type of proclivity to crime, not realizing that they (the Romans) are occupying the Palestinian territory and colonizing the community. It is easy to get away with murder when the system supports your particular policies and the justice system is not equal.

You will notice in the text, and you will also notice through history, that it is Hebrews during this time period who fill up the Roman jails. They have a higher arrest rate because there are more of them in that community being profiled by Romans. I'm not making this up, there was a stop-and-frisk policy that any Hebrew who looked at a Roman soldier wrongly could possibly be jailed or killed as a result.

There were failing schools in the Hebrew territory, and high unemployment, and race became a hindrance for growth and development, because Rome did not view Hebrews at the same level as those who were Roman citizens. They were seen as only three-fifths of a human being, and that seems to be a connection between what happened in the ancient period and what is happening today, because there are those who say that the majority of crimes that are committed in America are committed by people of color, people of African descent. But hold on. Wait a minute. Let me back up here so you understand what I'm trying to say.

The majority of crimes are not committed by people of African descent. The majority of crimes are committed by people of European descent. What is interesting is that we're always talking about black-on-black crime, but we never want to talk about white-on-white crime. We always want to frame it as if there was something wrong with one particular community. You see, the majority of convictions are African American, but the majority of arrests are European, which means that there is a justice system that treats us differently. It is two-tiered. One group is arrested but not convicted; another group is arrested and convicted for the same crime. If you check the FBI statistics, you will find that this is correct.

More people of color are convicted for a variety of reasons, specifically related to the belief within the racial imagination that Black people are already guilty as soon as we come into the system. One must understand here what is happening, because a system is at play. It is amazing that people are always talking about criminalization when talking about Black people. As soon as you go to the rural white area, where methamphetamine seems to be popular, everybody wants to talk about healthcare and how we can get help.

It's interesting that one group gets a healthcare response but the other group gets prison. I would say to you that this is not justice. This is just us. We have a two-tiered system that is happening, one system for those who are on meth and another system for those who utilize crack, one system for those who are on cocaine and another system for those who use heroin. Some people even try to say—even in this day and age—that there is no unfair system in place in America. "No, you Black people just need to pull yourself up by your bootstraps."

Let me break things down. There has been a system in place since we arrived on these shores in 1619. It was first known as slavery. Then after slavery, from 1863 to 1972, there was a system known as *peonage*. The sharecropping system was peonage, and it was the second tier of slavery. After 1863, you had men and women in the South whose labor was unfairly utilized through something known as the vagrancy laws.

Vagrancy laws stated that where two or three Black men gathered, you could be arrested if you did not have your papers to show where you lived and where you worked. If you did not have your papers, you could go to jail immediately. When you were imprisoned via peonage or traditional means of incarceration, you were sold to a private company. One of those companies was US Steel. US Steel would use your labor to rebuild the South after the Civil War. We built America before America was built, and we rebuilt the South after the South was torn down after the Civil War. From 1863 to 1972, you have the sharecropping system in America, and almost 500,000 people of African descent were imprisoned between the years of 1863 and 1972.

If you keep statistics, and you operate in Harvard, and you only read the statistics, it would appear that Black people are committing more crimes. But the reality is that there is a policy in place that is imprisoning people, and you have people writing policy to say that there is something wrong genetically and culturally with people of African descent. In 1972, when this system was abolished, a new system came into play when Richard Nixon became president. It was called the "war on drugs." As a result of the war on drugs, instead of getting the help that someone needs, we end up going after lower-level drug possession, and that is why our jails are now filled up with people who are black and brown.

We imprison more people in America than in China, Russia, or any other country in the industrialized world. I am here to let you know this isn't justice, this is just us. You can get away with murder when the system supports you. I don't want to stop you right there. I want to also give you some good news on how you change this system. We see here that Herod got away with murder. Herod had a system in place, and Herod put policies in place, and he had an entire army that was occupying a community, and as a result they ended up killing a whole lot of children.

Here is the good news right here. You will notice here that there is a messiah. There was a savior who was born, by the name of Jesus. You see Mary and Joseph were the parents of Jesus. Mary has Jesus—the Word that becomes flesh—in her belly, and Joseph is the adopted earthly father of Jesus.

I'm here to let you know that there's got to be some point in our moment and in our lives where some brothers stand up and adopt some children who are not your own, if we are to change this situation in our community. Not every child will be born through you. They will not have your DNA. If you look back over your life, you will know that there was somebody that did not have your DNA who poured into you. The reason you have reasonable success in your life is because somebody prayed, loved, supported, and disciplined you. Don't think it has to be someone from your own DNA. If it hadn't been for somebody else who poured into you, you would not be where you are right now.

We need men with a Joseph spirit. Here is the other thing. You see Mary and Joseph were together and had a baby here, but an angel came to Joseph and Mary, and they went down to Egypt.

Mary didn't say, "I'm going to go to church, you stay home." Joseph didn't say, "I'm going to go to church, you stay home." You see they were both on the same spiritual frequency. You cannot have a spirituality through proxy. You got to have your own spirituality, and when both people have a spirituality, then they're on the same level and they can raise a child that can be saved and become a leader for the entire nation. And that's why we need men and women, people who are willing to be on the same frequency.

Mary and Joseph are on the same frequency, and they are visited by the same angel, and here they go. They go down to Egypt. Here is the thing that, if we want to change the system, we've got to have parental preparation. We've got to have parents who can hear the voice of an angel, and we've got to be able to move into Egypt. Some of you are looking at me so weird like, "What are you talking about, Reverend, we've got to go into Egypt?"

Let me break it down historically. You must understand that the science and the technology of the day did not come from Rome, it came from Egypt. They were going to spend some time in Egypt, a safe time in Egypt, because there were other people who looked just like them in Egypt. If I'm going to hide from people chasing after me, I've got to hide around people who look just like me. You see it's easier for me to hide on the south side than it is in Elmhurst because there are more people who look like me. So they go to Egypt.

Wait a minute. It doesn't stop right there. Look at what happens here. They take them down to Egypt because there's excellence in Egypt. I want my child around other people who are doing great things. I want my child around the best in math and the best in architecture. I want them around some excellence of people who look just like them. They are now in Egypt, people who look just like them and there is excellence around their child. If there is gong to be parental preparation, we've got to ensure excellence among our children. If we are going to change the system, there must be excellence among our children.

I'm about to make somebody mad right now, but I don't care. We need to stop talking down to all the students right now. Don't you ever let anybody talk down to you. "What do you mean, Pastor, talk down to me?" Here's what I mean. Don't you ever let somebody tell you if you do well in school, you're acting white. Don't ever let anybody try to tell you that doing well is something wrong, that you're not Black enough if you're doing well in school. Tell them to shut up.

Let me take you down to Egypt and show you a pyramid. In order for you to build a pyramid you have to know the Pythagorean Theorem, which means that Pythagoras had to come down to Egypt if he wanted to know how to build a pyramid in the first place. Excellence is a part of who I am. I don't have to borrow it from somebody. There's excellence in my DNA. Stop all this stuff that says you are not Black if you do well in school. You are beautifully and wonderfully made by our God, and God wants you to be excellent.

It drives me crazy when people proudly say "I'm ghetto." You're ghetto? You don't even know what *ghetto* means. *Ghetto* describes a group of people who have been disempowered and live together in the same place. No one would want to "be ghetto" because you don't want to be disempowered by a system. Yet we are utilizing terms that have been given to us by other people and then defining ourselves by a system that does not care about who we are.

It is incumbent upon parents to have preparation so that your children can soar.

Mary and Joseph said, "We are going to take our child out of the system in Bethlehem because they're trying to take us out. So we're going down to Egypt, and we're going to learn to be unashamed about who we are and spend some time so that our child can develop in a system and in an area where he doesn't have to look over his shoulder if a Roman soldier is trying to take him out." There must be parental preparation if we are to change this system.

Here is the other thing that I love about this story. Jesus is born, and wise men from the East and shepherds from the community—both come to see about Jesus. The wise men are not indigenous to the Palestinian community, but they are coming to Jesus to celebrate what Jesus represents, even though they're not from that community. The shepherds are from the community, and they are also coming to see about Jesus.

Let me break it down. You have some highly educated folk from another neighborhood who are from east section, from the east side of this land. Then you have these people who are shepherds, right from the community. In order for us to change the system, we've got to make sure there's community partnership. There are going to be people who do not look like you, who are not from your community, who have a different experience from you. Guess what? We have the same commonality that we want to turn over some things and we want to see love, justice, and peace reign, and Jesus Christ is our Lord and our Savior.

Just because people look like you does not mean they are committed to what you're committed to. So you see that you have wise men that come from a different community and shepherds who come from the same community.

I believe it was W. E. B. Du Bois who said he was wrong when he said that a talented tenth would end up liberating the community. He rejected that idea, because it is not all bourgeois people who will liberate the community. You've got to build a coalition between people who are sweeping the street and those who've been to academia. When that coalition is built, something magnificent can happen in our land.

There must be a community partnership with people who do not look like you. There will be people who come from a different perspective. There will be people who speak a different language. They will not look like you. They will not have your classification. They will not define themselves as your race, but yet we have the same commonality that the wise men and the shepherds had.

The final thing is that for Jesus to show up there were already preachers who were preaching an alternative consciousness to the community. Walter Brueggemann speaks of an "alternative consciousness," which simply means that I am telling you what the world will be but is not yet (see *The Prophetic Imagination* [Minneapolis: Fortress Press, 2001]). That unto us a child is born. The government will be upon his shoulders. There is what some call the "pre-announcement" of Jesus (see Fulton J. Sheen, *Life of Christ* [New York: McGraw-Hill, 1950]). There is an announcement, a word, that prepares the people for hope. What does this mean? That simply means that there must be some prophetic preaching. The prophetic preaching just simply tells you that you've got to be in position for what God is going to do, even though God hasn't done it yet. You've got to act all the time as if God is about to do it.

You can't give up hope, because once you have a prophetic word in you, you know that God will eventually exalt every valley, that God will eventually bring every mountain low, that eventually the lion and the lamb will dance together, that eventually God will shift everything; but you've got to operate as if it's already happened. Another way to put it is this: you do not shout when the battle is over. In other words, you shout before the battle is over because you already know that God is still working, that God is not through with us yet.

That's what I love about Dr. King that day in Memphis, when he stood in that Pentecostal temple, and he stood before the people and said, "I've been to the mountaintop . . . I've seen the Promised Land. I may not get there with you. But I want you to know tonight, that we, as a people, will get to the Promised Land" (https:// kinginstitute.stanford.edu/king-papers/documents/ive -been-mountaintop-address-delivered-bishop-charles -mason-temple). He saw the glory of the Lord move in the lives of God's people, that we've got to begin to understand that we may not get there in this generation. There is another generation, the millennial generation, the younger generation that is doing things on another level, and it's our job to put them in position to do great things. But you've got to act like you're already there. You've got to move like God is still moving, because God does not operate under our timetable. When God got up this morning, the earth was not formed. When God goes to bed tonight, the earth will be no more. One day in God's eyes is 10,000 hours, and so we've got to operate as if God is already doing what God already promised to do, because God is not through with us yet.

How do you know God is not through with us yet? I've got to tell you. I turned on the TV the other night. I turned on CNN. I turned on MSNBC. I even turned on

Fox News. What messed me up when I turned on CNN, I saw some students at Stanford University. They had signs that said, "Black lives matter." I turned on MSNBC and I saw some students at Harvard University say, "Black lives matter." I even turned on Fox, and they had some students over in England saying, "Black lives matter." When I turned and looked all across the nation, I see Black, I see white, I see Latino, I see Asian, everybody with a sign "Black lives matter."

When I look at what's going on in the world, I know our God is not through with us yet. I know our God is still moving. God is moving in Chicago. God is moving in New York. God is moving in Ferguson. God is moving in Oakland. God is moving in India. God is moving in Australia. God is moving in South Africa. I know my God is still moving. Our God is moving. Our God is moving. Our God is still moving. God is moving. It's our job to operate in hope, even though you may have to operate against hopelessness, to operate in hope knowing that God is still moving. As I looked at the news and saw a bunch of students from the United Kingdom having a protest for people in Ferguson, that ain't nothing but God saying, "Black lives matter."

Many of those who are protesting don't even recognize that they have been pushed by the Spirit. They read a little Chomsky, some Gramsci, and know a little Marx, some liberation theology, but don't know they come out of a tradition where prayer warriors were sending up prayers back in 1863. Those prayers were embedded in the spirit soil, and all of a sudden, a generation was born, and they don't realize that they are benefitting from another generation who said, "This is wrong."

That's how movements are born. You don't create them. They are birthed by the Spirit. You can't control them. They're birthed by the Spirit of God. All of a sudden, different groups that would never connect are connecting with each other. You go to Ferguson, and you'll see the Black students with the evangelicals. The evangelicals would occupy Wall Street. They occupy Wall Street, standing with the environmentalists; the environmentalists are standing with the LGBTQ.

All these people standing together, who normally would be fighting one another, all of a sudden are saying, "But we do know that Black lives matter, and if Black lives matter, it means that brown lives matter." If brown lives matter, red lives matter. If red lives matter, yellow lives matter. If yellow lives matter, white lives matter. It means all lives matter, which is central to the gospel.

Herod, you can get away with murder for a season. Eventually, Shonda Rhimes knows that the season will conclude, and every show, no matter how good, will be cancelled. God operates at a level. You may think you get away with it on this show, but eventually God is going to catch up to you. Amen.